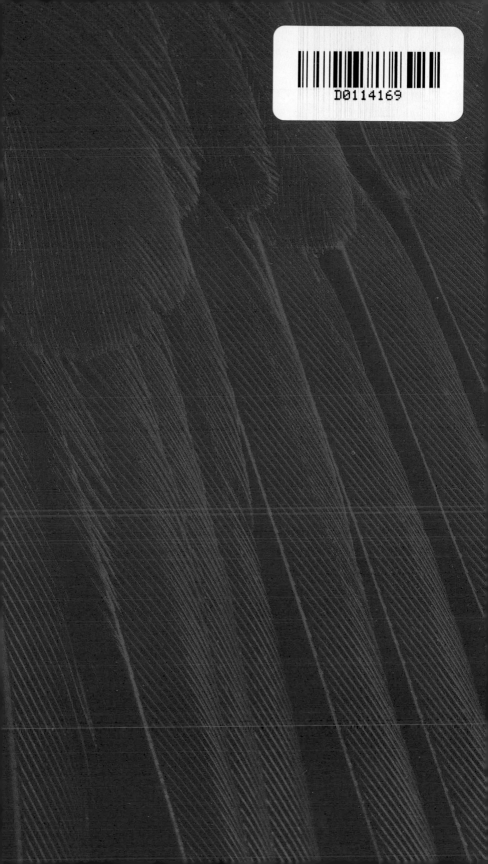

The Cardinal

NUMBER TWENTY-ONE
THE CORRIE HERRING HOOKS SERIES

JUNE OSBORNE

The Cardinal

PHOTOGRAPHS BY
BARBARA GARLAND

UNIVERSITY OF TEXAS PRESS

AUSTIN

LIBRARY OF CONGRESS
CATALOGING-IN-PUBLICATION DATA

Osborne, June, date.
    The cardinal / by June Osborne ; photographs by Barbara
Garland.—1st ed.
        p.   cm. — (The Corrie Herring Hooks series ; no. 21)
    Includes bibliographical references.
    ISBN 0-292-71147-6 (alk. paper)
    1. Cardinal-birds.   I. Title.   II. Series.
QL696.P2438O73   1992
598.8′83—dc20   91-48057

In the cardinal we have a rare combination of good qualities: brilliant plumage, a rich and pleasing voice, beneficial food habits, and devotion to its mate and family. Many of our best singers are not clothed in brilliant plumage, and many of our handsomest birds are not gifted musicians.

—Arthur Cleveland Bent,
Life Histories of North American Cardinals, Grosbeaks, Buntings, Towhees, Finches, Sparrows, and Allies

The female cardinal is soft grayish brown on the back, with tinges of red on crest, tail, and wings.

Contents

In richness of plumage, elegance of motion, and strength of song, this species surpasses all its kindred in the United States.

—John James Audubon

Author's Acknowledgments

*W*hen I was first asked to write a book on the Northern Cardinal, my answer was a resounding yes. I responded affirmatively, first, because I admire this beautiful red bird. I am drawn to it in an aesthetic sense because of its splashy color and its clear, whistled notes that have cheered my days, as a Christmas card verse goes, "in the dark of December." Second, I said yes because I have observed this bird not only through my own "bird windows" on countless occasions, but also in almost every state and province within its range north of the Rio Grande, and in parts of Mexico as well. I have tromped through its preferred habitat on more occasions than I care to admit.

I knew I could not accomplish this assignment alone. Because stunning photographs should be a part of such a book to enhance the text and to catch the eye of the reader, I chose Barbara Garland to be the photographer to illustrate this work. I shall be eternally grateful for her tireless efforts and her willingness to take one more photograph—no matter how hot the Texas sun—to illustrate a certain point. There is no telling how many rolls of film she exposed to get the collection of pictures you now hold in your hands.

Nature writers, researchers, bird-watchers, and ornithologists through the ages unknowingly contributed to this book through the storehouse of knowledge gathered in professional journals, books, magazine articles, and occasional papers. Janet Sheets, reference librarian at Baylor University's Moody Library in Waco proved to be expert in retrieving these documents. Many thanks to her and all her assistants.

I owe an enormous debt of gratitude to Baylor University biology professor Frederick R. Gehlbach, who so generously allowed me to use his unpublished notes, which were the result of twenty years of intensive research and observation of the Northern Cardinal in Waco. Additionally, I thank him for reading the manuscript in one of its earliest forms and for his many suggestions and words of encouragement along the way.

Thanks to Brian K. Loflin, my friend and business partner, for the range map, and to Sam, my son, for the other drawings.

I think almost all my friends and acquaintances had a cardinal story to tell. I drew from many of those stories in writing this book, especially from the experiences of Floyce Moon's first-graders. And to all those who opened their homes and property to Barbara and to me that we could observe (or photograph) a certain cardinal behavior—thanks to you all.

I am grateful to Mary Jane Camp for providing the Hawaiian expression for *cheer,* and to Nathan Stone for the many trans-Pacific phone calls it took to get from her (his Aunty Mele) just the right word with the appropriate number of syllables to fit the cardinal's most familiar song.

I would be remiss if I did not acknowledge the undying patience and understanding of my husband, Harold, throughout the almost two years I was absorbed in completing this project. I thank him for reading and rereading the manuscript and for giving constructive criticism that kept me on track.

The most difficult task I faced during the entire process was to keep from attributing anthropomorphic characteristics to this best-loved bird. It is hard not to attribute human characteristics to a bird that is loved by so many. So, my apologies to any reader who is offended by my occasional slip-ups.

Finally, Barbara and I hope that this combination of pen and camera has produced a work both informative and beautiful— one that will be enjoyed by people of all ages for a long time to come.

Photographer's Acknowledgments

To document the life history of the Northern Cardinal with pictures was a challenging assignment. Countless hours were spent sitting in a blind with the temperatures sometimes soaring. At other times the mercury plummeted.

In nature photography long hours of work do not always mean success. Some days I did not trip the shutter on my camera a single time. Other days, everything came together exactly right, and I exposed frame after frame of the beautiful cardinal.

During my ten years as a nature photographer, some of my most memorable shots have been taken as the direct result of a friend's help. This was also the case as I worked on *The Cardinal*. Many friends helped me in numerous ways. Billie Sue Mullen offered constructive suggestions regarding the project,

With his crimson plumage, the male cardinal is a striking subject to photograph.

for which I am deeply grateful. I also thank her for the countless ways she helped free my time for photography. Locating nests to photograph was a time-consuming activity. The following people helped: Bobbie Holland, Billy Lou Harper, John and Lavitha Dudley, Hollis Atkinson, Robert and Debbie Orr, and Leo and Sandra Dennis. Pam Moes made her backyard available to me on several occasions. Helen Hubler gave me access to her cardinal-rich farm and helped me construct a special bird feeder for photography, and John and Barbara Ingram made possible several shots on their property. Nell Smallwood and Mary Lee Bryan allowed me to erect a photo blind in their backyard, kept the feeder filled with sunflower seeds, and diligently reported cardinal activity to me.

June and I wish to thank Calvin Smith, Director of Baylor University's Strecker Museum in Waco, who graciously allowed us access to a museum specimen of a cardinal for the purpose of photographing the feathers to use as endpapers. We greatly appreciate this contribution and the assistance of his staff.

I thank Jim Mosley and Joe Irwin at Tom Padgitt, Inc., for technical assistance, and Tommie Suits for giving generously of his time to critique my slides.

Finally, my deepest gratitude goes to my mother, Gussie Garland, and my aunt, Nell Klinkman, for their support and encouragement.

Preface

I felt like a peeping Tom. I was watching a female cardinal busy at her toilette. I peered across a narrow inlet of water at the bottom of a wooded culvert and caught a glimpse of her reddish tail just as she flew from the water's edge. The thick tangle of tree roots protruding from the opposite bank almost hid her olive-gray sides from view.

As she snuggled in among the brambles to preen, I crouched behind a thorny bush to take full advantage of the show. Warily she looked in all directions to make sure no one was about, and then she proceeded to spread her red-tinged wings, like a geisha coyly unfolding her fan. Slowly, deliberately, she nibbled along the edge of each feather, until, grooming chores finished, she made her exit.

Still peeping through my thorny window, I was diverted by a flying burst of scarlet. The male cardinal, brilliant red plumage all awry, had just taken his turn at the bath. Too busy to groom every feather as the female had done, he simply shook himself fiercely all over, much the same as a dog often does to rearrange his fur. Then, with a "*chink,*" he flitted out of sight in the same direction as his mate.

Suddenly I realized that nature has not one window but many, and they are all around us.

Another day found me peering through a different sort of window—a beveled glass panel in a door leading from a spacious bedroom onto a redwood deck overlooking Lake Waco in Central Texas. This time I was seated in air-conditioned comfort inside a friend's home. Only inches outside this window was a seven-foot ficus in a large wooden planter. Nestled in its small branches was a loosely built nest. The face and body of a female cardinal were barely visible among the branches. She sat on the nest, quietly for the most part, her dark shoe-button eyes ever alert. Intermittently, she emitted a soft "*chink*" from her throat. After a few moments she moved to the side of the nest, and a wobbly, fuzzy head with bulging eyes appeared

[xiii]

beneath her—a tiny baby cardinal only three days out of the egg, my friend told me.

With a louder "*chink,*" the tawny female flew from the nest, and almost instantly a male cardinal appeared from somewhere in the surrounding woods to take his turn there. In his beak was a large green caterpillar, which he stuffed into the gaping mouth of the baby bird. I couldn't believe such a tiny bird could consume such a large caterpillar.

Still peering through the glass door, I wondered what would happen next. The patient father sat on the side of the nest while the hungry nestling gulped its meal. After a short while, the parent lowered his head into the nest and gathered in his bill a small white fecal sac deposited there by the nestling, and he carried it into the woods. Soon the mother returned to resume her vigil at the nest.

Another "window" gave me a dappled view as I gazed through the tiny openings in a camouflage net that covered a makeshift blind. Barbara Garland and I were watching four young cardinals as they devoured sunflower seeds on a friend's patio. The young birds, with varying shades of brown and red decorating their bodies, seemed to be of slightly different ages. One was almost golden brown and had no hint of red. I assumed this was a female. Another had tinges of red in its tail and wings, and I decided it was an older male cousin. The other two were plain brown all over with dark bills. It was impossible to determine their sex. They pecked at seeds that had spilled from the hanging feeder where House Finches were feeding above them.

One evening at dusk my spotting scope opened yet another window. As I scanned a lake shoreline, a crimson flash caught my eye. A male cardinal had just landed at water's edge. Slowly he dipped his beak to fill it with the refreshing liquid. He thrust his head back sharply so the water could trickle down his throat. In an instant he was gone. His tiny footprints were the only evidence he left behind. I was struck anew by his beauty and remarkable charm. Is it any wonder that the Northern Cardinal is one of America's favorite birds?

Through the pages of this book I hope to create many windows through which you may view the cardinal. First you will discover how the bird got its name and in what types of habitat and in what parts of the country it may be found. Through another of nature's "windows," you may view the seasons in the

life of this beautiful red bird. Beginning with January you will have your first close-up look when the male stakes out the territory in which he and his mate will breed and raise their young in the spring. You will watch as the pair go through their mating rituals, as they select their nesting site, and as the female constructs the nest. The birds, though sometimes facing adversity, will still be there, after having a second brood (and perhaps even a third and fourth), in midsummer.

You will learn about their favorite foods so that you can attract cardinals to your feeding stations. You will discover that during the fall molt, cardinals become secretive and almost totally silent while they exchange old feathers for new. Then suddenly their stark beauty reappears against a winter landscape when the tribe gathers, and flocks remain together until late December. When January rolls around once more, pairs of birds separate themselves from the flock, and a male cardinal surprises you with his long-awaited wake-up call on a cold winter morning. Then America's favorite "redbird" and his mate once again return to their chosen nesting ground—their land of beginning again—perchance, if you're lucky, in your own backyard.

Through another window you will see how the popularity of this flamboyant red bird affects American culture—as state symbol, athletic mascot, and object of art and literature. Finally, you will see why Big Red has become known as "the bird of Christmas."

The Cardinal

The Northern Cardinal is America's favorite "redbird."

The cardinal is one of the jewels of our bird-fauna, being incomparable in the combination of proud bearing and gaudy coloring, and unexcelled in certain qualities of its song. Few birds impart their haunts with such life, beauty, and poetry as this brilliant songster, one of the most famous among birds and highly prized by all bird lovers.

—Henry Nehrling (1896)

Introduction

*P*eople have been attracted to the beauty of the cardinal for centuries. Even in states and countries where the bird does not occur, it is known and admired. Among the first published pictures of a cardinal was a work in 1599 by Aldrovandi, the director of a botanical garden in Bologna, Italy. Since the bird was drawn from life, it apparently was captured in the New World and taken alive to the artist in Italy. Another early well-known drawing of the "Virginian Nightingale" appeared almost a century later in Francis Willughby's *Ornithologiae libri tres* (London, 1676). The bird's popularity, then, seems to be long-standing.

Cardinalis cardinalis is classified in the family Emberizidae. Some of America's finest songsters are in this family, including the Northern Cardinal.

The cardinal got its name from the Latin word *cardo*, "the hinge of a door." Figuratively this meant "important," or something upon which an object or an idea hinged or depended. The cardinal of the Roman Catholic Church is an important figure upon whose decisions matters of administration and policy depend, and he wears a red hat and robe. Hence Carollus Linnaeus, the famous eighteenth-century Swedish botanist known as the Father of Taxonomy, chose to ascribe the name *cardinal* to the bird whose plumage matches the radiant color of the papal robes of the church's cardinal. Through the centuries the name has stuck.

Throughout its range the Northern Cardinal has many colloquial nicknames. In the state of Virginia it is designated the "Virginia cardinal," "Virginia nightingale," and "Virginia redbird." Some Virginians have even gone so far as to call it an FFV—a member of one of the First Families of Virginia.

In the bluegrass state it is called the "Kentucky cardinal." John James Audubon, one of America's most renowned naturalists, once lived in Henderson, Kentucky, where Audubon State Park was named in his honor. Here two bronze plaques

Range of the Northern Cardinal.
Map by Brian K. Loflin/The Nature Connection.

commemorate the early explorer, ornithologist, and artist. Each of the plaques is decorated with images of cardinals, one of Audubon's favorite songbirds. In describing the cardinal in his journals, he said, "In richness of plumage, elegance of motion, and strength of song, this species surpasses all its kindred in the United States." In other localities the bird is known as "cardinal grosbeak," "cardinal bird," "Big Red," "topknot redbird," and "crested redbird." However, the most popular moniker by which this scarlet beauty is affectionately known is simply "redbird."

The cardinal is a year-round nonmigratory resident from the Dakotas, southern Ontario, and Nova Scotia south to the Gulf Coast, and from southern Texas westward through Arizona and southward through Mexico as far as Guatemala and Honduras. The Northern Cardinal was introduced in Hawaii in 1929 and now is well established there. It also occurs in southwestern California and in Bermuda as an introduced species.

In the *Field Guide to Mexican Birds,* Roger Tory Peterson and Edward Chalif mention the Pacific Coast form *Cardinalis carnea* that ranges from Colima to Oaxaca. Formerly it was considered a distinct species known as the Long-crested Cardinal. Most authorities, however, now agree it is not.

South America claims seven species of birds with *cardinal* in their names. Only one of them, the Vermilion Cardinal (*Cardinalis phoeniceus*), is in the same genus as our familiar Northern Cardinal. It has a limited range in the northern extremes of Venezuela and Colombia. The male is all red with a long upright crest. The female has brown upperparts and a small red crest. Her underparts are ochraceous buff. The other six South American "cardinals" are the Yellow Cardinal (*Gubernatrix cristata*), whose range includes most of Argentina and Uruguay; the Red-crested Cardinal (*Paroaria coronata*), which lives throughout Bolivia, Paraguay, Uruguay, and most of Argentina; the Red-cowled Cardinal (*Paroaria dominicana*), found within the northeastern portions of Brazil; the Red-capped Cardinal (*Paroaria gularis*) of northwestern South America; the Crimson-fronted Cardinal (*Paroaria baeri*) of interior Brazil; and, finally, the Yellow-billed Cardinal (*Paroaria capitata*).

Their range extends from just north of Paraguay southward through the northern half of Argentina.

Granted, all these exotic South American "cardinals" are colorful, but none compares with America's favorite flamboyant redbird. Paul R. Ehrlich said it well: "Birds are, hands down, the most colorful terrestrial vertebrates—only insects and coral reef fishes rival them among animals." The cardinal has to be close to the top of the list of most colorful birds. Indeed, many people have become much interested in *all* birds by first being attracted by the beauty of the cardinal.

It doesn't take a bird expert to identify a male Northern Cardinal. Whether a person knows much about birds or not, almost everyone who lives within its range recognizes the male cardinal's brilliant red plumage, its crest, and its clearly whistled songs. From his perky topknot, which he raises and lowers at will, to the tip of his long slender tail, the male cardinal is covered with crimson feathers. The feathers on his back and scapulars are edged with brown or gray, giving his back a somewhat duller appearance than the rest of him. His iris is dark reddish brown, brown, or hazel. A roguish black mask surrounds his strong, cone-shaped coral-red bill. Even his feet and legs are dark red.

By contrast, his female counterpart is soft grayish brown on the back. She shows variable tinges of red on her crest, tail, and short rounded wings. There is an area of darker feathers around her bill, but nothing like the male's distinctive black mask. Her underparts are warm pinkish brown, and her bill is about the same color as the male's.

Since the male weighs slightly more than the female, he may appear to be a little larger than she is in any given pair. The average weight of the male is 45.4 grams; that of the female, 43.9 grams.

The unattractive juvenile looks as if someone made a mistake when applying its color. The only thing about it that is cardinal-like is its shape. Its identity is sometimes a mystery to those not familiar with the somewhat plain markings. It is browner overall than the female and has a blackish bill. Its crest is not quite as long as that of its parents. The plumage of the immature male is tinged with red. When fall arrives, the young cardinals of both sexes begin to molt, and one month later, after acquiring their first winter's plumage, they look exactly like their parents.

Cherokee legend has it that the cardinal was originally an all-brown bird, much like the juvenile just described. In the story, the little brown bird was most unhappy with his dingy feathers. All the other birds of the forest were brightly colored, and they made fun of the ugly one. One day in his wanderings he came upon a wolf that had been tricked by a raccoon. While the wolf was sleeping, the raccoon placed mud packs on his eyes so that when he awoke he couldn't open them. When the brown bird saw the plight of the wolf, he befriended him by pecking the mud away from his eyes. The wolf was so grateful that he rewarded the unattractive bird for his kindness by telling him where there was a rock with streaks of bright red paint running through it. According to the legend, the bird found the rock and painted himself. Ever since, he has been red and considered the most beautiful bird in the forest.

There are two other all-red birds of the North American forest that might be mistaken for the cardinal: the Summer Tanager (*Piranga rubra*) and the Hepatic Tanager (*Piranga flava*). Both are slightly smaller than the cardinal. The Summer Tanager averages 7¾ inches in length and the Hepatic Tanager 8 inches, but the cardinal—typically 8¾ inches—is longer. Although the observer may think at first that these birds are cardinals, he soon sees that the tanagers have no crest and no black mask; too, they are migratory. The Summer Tanager lives in the southern United States and the Hepatic Tanager in the Southwest only during breeding season. The Northern Cardinal is present in those regions year-round.

Next of kin to the cardinal is the Pyrrhuloxia (*Cardinalis sinuatus*), a resident of the Southwest. It is sometimes called the "Texas cardinal." Its song is similar to that of the Northern Cardinal, and its body has the general shape and size of the cardinal. When seen in silhouette the two may seem identical.

Cherokee legend has it that the cardinal was originally an all-brown bird, much like this juvenile.

In some localities the cardinal is known as "topknot redbird" and "crested redbird."

Close inspection reveals that the male Pyrrhuloxia is an exquisite shade of gray overall, with red on his face where the cardinal is black. He has red in the tip of the crest and on the wings and a generous spilling of rose color on the belly and tail. His bill is orange-yellow in contrast to the cardinal's coral-red. The female Pyrrhuloxia is mostly gray and shows very little, if any, red anywhere.

Where the territories of *Cardinalis cardinalis* and *Cardinalis sinuatus* overlap—in southwestern Texas, southern New Mexico, southeastern Arizona, and in Mexico—a bird-watcher may have difficulty in determining which is which, because their songs as well as their silhouettes are similar. One must carefully examine the face and bill of the cardinal look-alike, Pyrrhuloxia. A surprising difference exists in the shapes of their bills. The Pyrrhuloxia looks as if it has been in a fight with a heavyweight boxing champion—and lost. Its parrotlike bill is thick and strongly curved, giving it the appearance of having been almost flattened.

The Northern Cardinal is found in a variety of settings, from the Everglades of South Florida to the evergreens of the North to the arid desert lands of the Southwest and Mexico. The cardinal has adapted to habitats over wide areas in both temperate and subtropical climates. The species seems as much at home in a woodland edge or desert shrub, in a streamside thicket or dingy chaparral, as in an elaborately landscaped New England urban garden or the preserves of the Deep South.

Have you ever wondered where cardinals go each day after they feed voraciously in your backyard? From early morning until late evening they are frequent diners at feeding stations. They linger awhile on the ground or on low feeding trays, fill themselves with sunflower seeds you have placed there for them, and then disappear. Where do they go? If you followed the low, pumping flight of one, you would find yourself in a surprising assortment of places.

If you live in the South your cardinal might lead you into a pine forest with deciduous undergrowth. In Florida's Everglades I followed a cardinal onto Snake Bight Trail, which led me deep into a mangrove swamp. There thick swarms of mosquitoes soon forced me to give up pursuit of the bird.

In the Southwest and in Mexico you might follow your winged guide into desert shrub or chaparral as I once did. Near San Fernando in Tamaulipas, I saw a male cardinal with an insect in its mouth. I assumed it was about to feed its young. Curiosity led me to try to locate the nest to photograph it, but it was not to be. Instead of locating the nest, I soon found myself knee-deep in thorny vegetation. I could go no farther.

In other places you may find yourself in a brushy border, in thick tangles of greenbrier, in a streamside thicket, or possibly even on a country roadside. Roadsides can be quite dangerous for the bird if it lands too close to the roadway. Thousands of birds are inadvertently killed each year by passing cars. Once photographer Barbara Garland found a dead female cardinal beside a country road. She stopped to watch when she noticed the bird's mate flying back and forth above the lifeless form.

So you see, if you *could* follow your favorite redbird when it leaves your garden, you would find it at home in a number of interesting and varied habitats. Soon you would realize there *is* life—and death—for the cardinal outside your backyard.

To everything there is a season, and a time to every purpose under the heaven.

—Ecclesiastes 3:1

PART I

Seasons in the Life of the Cardinal

The male bursts into flight in a blur of crimson.

A bird's song is an audible fence. It announces to rivals that the singer's territory is taken and will be defended.

—Paul A. Johnsgard

January: Establishing Territory

On a bleak morning in January, one may awaken to the sound of a male cardinal in full song. Indeed, this is the season in the life of the cardinal that may best be characterized by song. This is the time during which the bird constructs an audible barrier that designates a few acres as his territory. Just as the bricklayer constructs a wall, laying brick on brick, the male cardinal delimits the invisible boundaries of his territory, laying note on note.

Territory is defined as any area defended by a bird against other birds of its own kind. It may be roughly classified into two categories: breeding territory and nonbreeding territory. The commonest type is breeding territory—that used for mating, nesting, and feeding of the adults and the young. Once a pair of birds claims a territory, they usually remain there at least until their offspring are independent. Nonbreeding territory may be used for foraging away from the breeding grounds or for nighttime roosting—a place to sleep during the winter months, for example. This type is usually defended just as fiercely as the breeding territory.

Territory size varies widely among bird species, from mere inches to several miles. Extremes may be illustrated by the average thirty-six square miles defended by the Golden Eagle and the one square foot defended by the Common Murre. The eagle's territory is multipurpose and is spread out because its chief food—small mammals—is thinly dispersed over a large area. The murre is a seabird that nests in large colonies on rocky ledges overlooking the sea. Its territory is so small that sometimes birds touch one another while sitting on their nests. Northern Cardinals, in comparison, defend an area from less than two to ten acres in size. In this plot of ground there may be other species of birds—mockingbirds, wrens, or jays, for example—but there will be only one pair of cardinals.

Cardinals, and other birds, use song to proclaim their territory. In a study of cardinals conducted in the Woodway

While in full song, the cardinal raises its crest, giving the bird character and revealing its full beauty.

Ravine, Waco, Texas, from 1965 to 1990, biology professor Frederick R. Gehlbach discovered that territorial singing begins between January 8 and 22. Arthur Cleveland Bent describes the cardinal as a persistent singer throughout most of the year. Amelia R. Laskey says that full song by the males usually extends from February to September, and by the females, from March until July or August.

No matter what the date, it is pleasant indeed to awake on an early January morning when a Northern Cardinal's jubilant song invites you to see the sunrise. The sound is especially welcome when you remember that it has been a long, long time since the sweet voice was heard. The birds have been almost totally silent since they went into their postbreeding molt—the time when they lose all their worn-out feathers and replace them with a fine new set after nesting duties are completed.

While in full song, the cardinal raises its crest, giving the bird character and revealing its full beauty. On a January morning the casual listener may not realize that the bold and beautiful crimson male, dressed in his splendid new winter coat, is actually constructing an audible fence with his singing just as surely as if he were building a wall. Though his barrier is invisible to the human eye, it is quite real to other male cardinals competing for territory. To them the singer is announcing that these few acres are preempted by him, and interlopers should not cross over into his space.

Song is only one element in avian communication. Basically birds have two modes: (*a*) visual displays, or body language, which I will discuss later, and (*b*) vocal displays, generally classified in two categories—songs and call notes.

Song mainly consists of syllables or sounds consistently repeated in a specific pattern. These songs are usually sung, with some exceptions, only by territorial males during breeding season. The Northern Cardinal female is one of those exceptions. She is as accomplished a singer as her male counterpart. Her song is softer than his, is sung somewhat less frequently, and is often used to defend their territory against invasions by other female cardinals. Her songs and call notes also bond her to her mate.

When do cardinals sing? One may be heard singing with as much vigor on a subfreezing day during a Minnesota winter as on a blazing hot day in the Southwest's summer heat. Some birds, such as the Carolina Wren, sing year-round, but this is not the norm. Most birds in the Temperate Zone virtually end their singing after the nesting season, especially during their postbreeding molt. Frequently during this off period, however, some birds, including the cardinal, sing what is called a soft "whisper" or muted song. With audibility limited to no more than about twenty yards, sometimes this whisper song is too soft to be heard, which leads bird-watchers to think the birds are not singing at all.

Some birds sing all day long and into the night. The Northern Mockingbird is notorious for being a tireless nocturnal virtuoso. It may surprise some cardinal devotees to discover that cardinals, too, occasionally sing at night. I have been awakened at 1:00 A.M. on many a spring night when the cardinals of our neighborhood joined the chorus of the mockingbird's nightly recital.

Henry Nehrling, a writer of the nineteenth century, said that when cardinals hear mockingbirds from far and near rivaling in their singing, "the Cardinals cannot withstand the temptation of joining the chorus of this nocturnal concert. At first one utters a few notes, which slowly increase in power, becoming louder, fuller, and more varied. . . . I have heard this incomparably enchanting concert of Nature not only when the moon poured her light on the landscape, but also during very dark nights." Nehrling's favorite place in which to observe cardinals was along the Texas coast in April. He said, "The spring and summer nights in the Gulf region are indescribably charming and bewitchingly beautiful when Mockingbirds and Cardinals join in their fascinating night concerts."

John Burroughs noted in one of his journals, "Along the Potomac I have heard the Virginia cardinal whistle so loudly and persistently in the treetops above, that sleeping after four o'clock (A.M.) was out of the question."

No matter when they sound off, the quality of vocalizations in different species of birds ranges from the sublime to the ridiculous. What could be more sublime than the ethereal flutelike notes of a Wood Thrush floating through the eerie half-light of dawn or dusk in an eastern forest? Or what could be more ridiculous than the "*Gallump! Gallump! Gallump!*" of an American Bittern hiding within the reeds of a marsh? To me the sweet-voiced song of the Northern Cardinal falls very near the sublime end of the spectrum of avian vocalizations. Some observers think the notes of the cardinal are almost equal to those of the Nightingale, the bird considered the "sweetest feathered minstrel of Europe."

The cardinal has many different songs. Indeed, at one time it was a much sought-after caged bird—even more so than canaries—because its plumage and musical ability are equally brilliant. In the nineteenth century, cardinals were trapped by the thousands in the South during winter and taken to markets in the North. In addition, thousands were shipped annually to Europe where they were regarded as caged birds of the highest rank. Nehrling wrote about this in 1896: "This glory of our bird-fauna deserves everywhere careful protection and fostering. Stringent laws should be passed by the legislatures of the Southern States for the protection of birds, and these laws should be strictly enforced." Thankfully, since the Migratory Bird Treaty Act was enacted in 1918, our native birds are protected by federal laws. Now the birds and their songs can be enjoyed only as they were meant to be—in the wild—and unconfined.

Widely distributed species, such as the cardinal, often have pronounced local variations or accents in their song much like the distinctive dialects spoken by people in different parts of the country. Although the cardinal has two dozen or more variations in its song, each one has a typically cardinal quality no matter which dialect the bird is using. Something about the voice quality and the general phraseology leaves no doubt in the mind, no matter where listeners are when they hear it, that this is a cardinal singing. Some visitors to Hawaii are surprised and delighted upon their first arrival in the islands when they hear a Northern Cardinal's rich familiar song. Of course, there, it may be interpreted by the natives as sounding more like "*Le'a-le'a!*" (the Hawaiian word for "cheer" or "joy") than "*What cheer-cheer-cheer!*"

Call notes are normally short sounds that lack a specific pattern. They include all vocalizations made by birds that cannot be described as song. The most familiar call note made by cardinals is the short, metallic "*chink*" or "*chip*" often heard around backyard feeders. This note may be uttered in many different situations to convey different messages, such as an aggressive warning to an intruding male. Or the bird may simply be trying to stay in touch with its mate, to say it is going to roost, for instance. Or the call note may be given as an alarm to warn the other of some lurking danger such as the presence of a predator.

During fall and winter I often hear that warning call near my backyard feeders when a Sharp-shinned Hawk suddenly appears there to look for an easy meal of some small unsuspecting bird. Simply by the cardinal's tone of voice, I know it signals the presence of the hawk, and certainly the other birds know, because they immediately scatter for cover. (Gehlbach reports that a male cardinal recently released from banding was caught by a Sharp-shin, but the feisty cardinal fought off the hawk in five seconds flat. Could it be that the cardinal was prepared for a fight because of the warning calls of some other bird?) In short, the call note serves a dual purpose: to convey a variety of messages between mates and to warn other birds about intruders.

We humans tend to listen to bird songs with our aesthetic sense, and whether we understand their meaning or not, we enjoy what we hear. Although countless studies have examined what motivates a bird to sing, they all seem to indicate that males' songs have two primary functions: (*a*) to attract a female of the same species and (*b*) to drive away other males of the same species. It's as simple as that. In other words, the male singer is saying, "I am an available male who would like to have a mate" and "I own this territory from which I sing, and I dare any male of like species to invade these boundaries!" The female bird that sings is saying, in essence, "I like what I hear, I accept your invitation, and all other females of my kind may as well stay away."

Each and every species has its own unique song that is different from the songs of every other species. Even individual birds within a species have their own unique songs. Some authors claim that each song is as distinctive as a fingerprint. With practice and experience, a person can learn to recognize birds by their songs. Knowledgeable birders don't even have to *see* the birds to know what species are present. The songs give them a prescriptive clue to the birds' identities.

Novices, on the other hand, may encounter utter confusion, when on a spring morning they stroll through the park and try to differentiate between the diverse warbler songs that surround them. They should not despair. Records, tapes, and compact discs can aid anyone learning to recognize bird songs. The Laboratory of Ornithology at Cornell University in Ithaca, New York, and ABA Sales in Colorado Springs, Colorado, offer such recordings.

Even though the casual human observer may not be able to tell the difference between the songs of a Carolina Wren and a Northern Cardinal, the birds know the difference. Some researchers believe that a bird responds only to the song of its own species. According to them, a cardinal will not respond even to a well-executed imitation of its song when given by a mockingbird. Other ornithologists claim that a cardinal will respond to a whistled imitation of its territorial call. At any rate, since most bird songs are species-specific, the difference in the songs ensures that females will mate only with members of their own species and thus prevent hybridization.

Have you noticed that different species of birds prefer different heights from which to sing? Some songbirds occasionally sing from the ground. The American Robin is one of these. But most birds prefer a perch that is high above the ground. Cardinals prefer the lofty places like treetops and high utility wires. According to the section of the country in which you observe them, they may be seen singing from atop a tall pine tree in the Southeast or from a giant saguaro in the Sonoran Desert.

The cardinals in our neighborhood in Central Texas, for example, prefer the TV antenna on the rooftop of our next-door neighbor's house. From there, on most mornings from mid-winter through the summer, our resident male redbird delivers a wake-up call to the entire neighborhood: "*What cheer-cheer-cheer!*" he calls. And from somewhere in the backyard his mate answers, matching his song, phrase for phrase, "*What cheer-cheer-cheer!*" This duetting is called "countersinging" and occurs mainly in permanently paired species in which both sexes stay together year-round. It strengthens the bond between them and lets others of their kind know that this territory is occupied and will be defended at all costs.

Sometimes a male from an adjoining territory countersings, following and matching the phrases of the first male. This type of countersinging between males is often interspersed with flights into one another's space. When this happens, the intruding male is chased away by the resident male.

Occasionally, an unmated female attempts to invade another's territory. When this occurs, the resident female chases her away while her mate observes the action passively. Cardinals usually are tolerant of the opposite sex and do not become involved in joint efforts with their mates to drive off intruders.

It takes a good imagination to put words to the musical notes of birds. Numerous writers have described the songs of cardinals in various ways. "*What cheer-cheer-cheer!*" is a popular interpretation of one of the most familiar of cardinal songs.

Overall, a cardinal's song is a variable series of loud, rich, whistled notes sometimes sounding like, "*Wheer, wheer, wheer. Whoit, whoit, whoit, whoit.*" The first three notes descend in pitch, and the "*whoit*" notes rise sharply and are delivered more rapidly.

Another series of phrases may be interpreted as "*Hew whoit whoit whoit,*" or "*Whit-chew, whit-chew, whit whit whit*" or "*Cue, cue, cue.*"

At other times we hear "*Birdy, birdy, birdy!*" or "*Purty, purty, purty!*" as if the bird is admitting to the world he knows how beautiful he is. No matter what interpretation one ascribes to the songs of the cardinal, hearing "*What cheer-cheer-cheer!*" does help brighten an otherwise bleak day in the dead of winter.

The fact remains that whether perched on utility wires strung alongside busy highways or in the lacy branches of cypress trees that line a pristine river, the brilliant red of a male Northern Cardinal and the cheery notes of its song capture our attention.

Have you ever wondered how long it takes a bird to sing its song? In 1958, Charles A. Hartshorne discovered that the primary song of most of the songbirds takes less than four seconds to execute. *Primary song* is defined as the vocalization most commonly heard in spring and summer when the bird is on its nesting territory. The longest fixed primary bird song he found was that of the Winter Wren, which lasted from eight to ten seconds. Hartshorne also found that the songs of the cardinal fall in the midlength category, varying from 1.8 to 4.2 seconds. Of course, these brief renditions are repeated at several-second intervals, giving the listener the impression of a much lengthier song.

In most species of birds, only the male sings, and only during the brief breeding season of spring and summer. But among cardinals, male and female sing equally well. And, although most authors report that the cardinal sings year-round, I have observed that the ones around our home are almost totally silent from the time they begin their fall molt until late December or early January. If they sing at all during this period, it is the soft whisper song described earlier. Consequently, one-third of the year we are deprived of their beautiful full song. That is one reason why the sound of a cardinal's clear tones is so welcome against the backdrop of a cold, drab morning in January—the time of beginning again for America's favorite redbird—when he builds his invisible boundary wall, laying note on note.

Birds increase their visits to feeders in harsh weather, particularly after snowfalls and ice storms that make natural foods inaccessible.

—Paul Ehrlich

Each species has its own method of courtship and breeding, a ritualized strategy for survival so deeply imbued in the genes that no individual bird has to figure out how it ought to proceed.

—Paul A. Johnsgard

February and March: Winter Feeding, Range Expansion, and Courtship

*T*he February sky was dark gray and looked ominous as sundown approached. By bedtime a cold rain began to fall. A heavy covering of snow, unusual for Central Texas, surprised my family and me the next morning. Suddenly, it seemed that the bird feeders in our backyard became *the place to visit* by all the birds for miles around. Birds that my family and I normally do not see on a daily basis joined the cardinals, Blue Jays, and Carolina Chickadees.

That day we observed a Brown Thrasher who came at least three times to bathe in the slush in the birdbath that had the consistency of an icy drink from the neighborhood convenience store. Dark-eyed Juncos by the dozens were at the back of the garden. A Harris' Sparrow and a White-crowned Sparrow, usually birds of the open country, on that day found sustenance in suburbia. A Rufous-sided Towhee scratched like a chicken in the tray of scratch feed.

I spent the entire day filling and refilling feeders and defrosting the birdbath every hour or so. The rest of the family, when they weren't helping me or playing in the snow, spent their time looking out the window at the ever-changing bird scene. The crimson robes of the male cardinals were by far the most stunning of this colorful array against the white background.

Winter Feeding and Range Expansion

Scenes such as the one just described are not unusual in backyards all across the land during the colder months of the year, and so we dub this the season for backyard bird-watchers to pour on the food for our bird friends.

There is no doubt that winter feeding stations are beneficial to birds, especially in the northern regions of the United States where weather can be extreme. They supply a food source when natural food is covered by ice or snow. However, a person doesn't really need a motive for feeding birds other than wanting to see them up close. And what better way to do this than to offer them food right outside the windows? At any rate, feeding birds is an interesting pastime that benefits not only the avian species, but also *Homo sapiens*, who so enjoys a close look at feathered wildlings.

At the age of seventy-four, my mother started feeding birds in her backyard. At that time she was so crippled with arthritis that she could not go out on field trips to see the birds she loved to watch. My family and I gave her a bird feeder and kept her supplied with seeds so the birds would come to her. The last four years of her life she spent many a pleasant hour sitting in her breakfast room and watching the birds outside the window. My youngest son was four years old when he first took an interest in watching the activity at our "bird window."

Why does feeding backyard birds have such a wide appeal to people of all ages? The answer may be that it brings life to the scene outside and adds color to our lives. Marjorie Valentine Adams, in *A Gift of Birds*, explains the appeal this way: "Birds do many of the things humans do, as we may see ourselves mirrored in some of their habits and actions. They can be comical, joyous, tender, fierce or puzzling, matching almost any basic human behavior."

I suppose people have been giving birds handouts as long as people have been watching birds. The practice came into vogue in the late 1800s, when numerous books were published on the subject of feeding birds. In his 1896 publication, Henry Nehrling said that cardinals came in numbers of five to ten to a feeding place he had arranged for various birds in the woods bordering his house in Missouri.

Feeding birds in North America began to increase dramatically in the early 1950s. Since then the practice has grown so rapidly that an estimated 82.5 million Americans now spend more than one-half billion dollars annually just to feed the birds. That means nearly half of the population over sixteen years of age feeds birds as a hobby. The data collected by the

U.S. Fish and Wildlife Service indicate that over 20 million new people began feeding wild birds between 1980 and 1985. Attracting birds to our yards with feeding stations is now second only to gardening in popularity as an outdoor pastime. New Englanders are our most dedicated providers, with no less than 40 percent of the households of Amherst, Massachusetts, offering winter food for birds. One study showed that, overall, one in three North American households makes available an average of sixty pounds of supplemental seed each year. That's a lot of bird seed! For your money, one of the best-nourishing seeds to buy for your backyard birds is the small black oil sunflower seed. It provides more nutrition than the larger striped seeds. Cardinals love them, and so do numerous other species.

Some authorities believe this increased interest in winter feeding has expanded the range of certain species of birds. For example, in Audubon's day (1785–1851) the cardinal was considered a southern bird and was rarely seen as far north as Philadelphia. By 1895 its range reached the Great Lakes, and by 1910 the cardinal was in southern Ontario and along the southern portion of the Hudson River. In more recent years, cardinals have become common backyard breeding birds as far north as some parts of southern Canada. During the 1989 Christmas Bird Count, an annual census that attempts to determine the early winter distribution of our native birds, counters in Ontario tallied 6,303 Northern Cardinals in some sixty areas. That same year, 3 cardinals were counted in Manitoba, 4 in Nova Scotia, 7 in New Brunswick, and 125 in the province of Quebec. (These figures in no way reflect the total number of cardinals in these areas. They merely indicate the number counted on a particular day in those particular areas.)

Other authorities explain the cardinal's range expansion by temperature and moisture conditions in certain parts of the country. For example, Terry Root, in her analysis of Christmas Bird Count data spanning the winters from 1962/1963 through 1971/1972, discovered that, to the north, the cardinal in winter is found where the average minimum January temperature is above five degrees Fahrenheit. And, according to her findings, the western edge of the main wintering area of cardinals is influenced by moisture, with the species frequenting only those regions that receive more than sixteen inches of annual precipitation.

One of the most intriguing theories offered for the cardinal's push northward is one espoused by Roger Tory Peterson, author, bird artist, and guru of North American bird-watchers. Formerly the cardinal's range was bounded on the east by the Hudson River. With that in mind, consider Peterson's idea that it was the building of the George Washington Bridge in 1931 that enabled the cardinals to cross the Hudson. He explains that since they are not highly migratory birds, it is reasonable to assume that after the bridge was built cardinals were able to cross the river without having to make long sustained flights. Now they can make their way slowly across the river by resting from time to time on the struts of the bridge.

John V. Dennis, well-known authority on feeding birds, agrees with those who say the cardinal's northward expansion has largely been made possible by the availability of food at feeding stations. He says, "Ability to adapt to a variety of habitats, and especially to advantages offered by humans, is a prime factor in the cardinal's success." The truth is, no one really knows for sure why cardinals now occur where once they did not. Whatever the reasons, that brilliant flash of red is now one of the most common and most welcome sights around feeders throughout the bird's range.

Indeed, the Northern Cardinal, more than any other bird, has come to symbolize bird feeding. A buyer for a major bookstore chain once told a publisher that he would not buy a particular bird book for sale in his stores because it did not have a cardinal on the cover. How many books have you seen on the subject of attracting birds that have a picture of a male cardinal on the front? I counted six in my own personal library. The books without them would be easier to count. Or how many bags of birdseed do you see on your grocer's shelves without an artist's rendition of a cardinal decorating the package?

Granted, the bright color of this bird attracts the reader's or shopper's attention, but the cardinal won its place in advertising in ways that have nothing to do with color. It is one of the first birds to appear at feeders in the morning, sometimes before daylight, and one of the last to leave in the evening, often after dark. Incidentally, Texas bird-watcher Fred Gehlbach suspects this may be the reason cardinals are highly susceptible to predation by Eastern Screech-Owls, who feed at those times of day. He reports that cardinals are the second most common resident species eaten by screech owls (behind the House Sparrow), and 71 percent of these are males, a statistically significant number indicating male boldness. He cites one example of a male cardinal that was banded on February 9, 1978, and found as stored food in a screech owl nest only a thousand feet away a little more than a year later on May 3, 1979.

The reward for maintaining feeding stations throughout the summer months as well as winter comes when cardinal parents bring their offspring there to teach them the advantages of a readily available food supply. It is feasible to assume that since some cardinals have as many as three, four, or five broods of young in one nesting season (depending on the area of the country), the enjoyment of watching them at close range may be sustained over an extended period of time throughout the summer months.

I keep feeders well stocked throughout the year, and by the first of August each year I have usually already seen the juveniles of at least three broods from the same pair of cardinals. It is interesting to watch them, because soon you can recognize the different individuals by the way they act or by a feather that is out of place or some other distinguishing feature. Once I observed a juvenile cardinal that fed on the ground every day until he discovered above him the hanging feeder that contained more seeds than he could find on the ground. As soon as he made the discovery he started going directly to the feeder without first checking out the ground-level seed supply. He dared any other species, such as the ubiquitous House Sparrow, even to alight on the feeder. It became his own personal property. Over a period of several days I observed that the only other bird he would tolerate on the feeder while he was there was an adult female. I assumed she was his own mother.

Cardinals' short, heavy beaks crack seeds with strong adductor muscles that enable them to handle larger and tougher seeds that birds with smaller bills cannot crack. The grooved upper mandible holds the seed while the sharp-edged lower mandible moves forward and crushes and husks the seed. The bird then swallows the inner nutmeat.

Popular belief has it that cardinals eat only sunflower seeds, but this is not true. They accept with equal fervor cracked corn; white millet; nutmeats of all kinds; the seeds of squash, watermelon, pumpkin, and cantaloupe; and other grains, such as wheat and barley.

Sylvia Montroy, a writer who lives in New Jersey, relates a charming story of her family's discovery of the cardinal's affinity for squash seeds. She recalls that one day while preparing acorn squash for dinner, she decided, on a whim, to place the seeds in a pan on the deck within six feet of a sliding glass door to their family room. For several months the seeds remained untouched. Finally, a male cardinal investigated the pan's contents and liked what he tasted. His mate soon joined him, and after that the Montroy family ate acorn squash far more often than they would have chosen, just so they could provide the birds with their preference in treats.

Montroy said she soon realized that in order to keep the cardinals continually supplied with the seeds her family would have to eat squash every day. Since they were not prepared to do that, she started ordering the seeds through a seed catalog. Though she paid a high price for them, she said it was worth every cent, because when breeding season rolled around her family was treated to an educational aspect of the project she had not counted on—the parents teaching their offspring independence. One day a fledgling could not figure out what to do with the large uncracked seed its parent placed in its mouth. After rotating it in its beak, scrubbing it against the deck floor, and dropping and retrieving it time after time without success, the young bird finally gave up and in desperation ate a geranium petal from a potted plant nearby instead. Squash, anyone?

Some cardinals have been observed feeding on nectar. Mary W. Wible of Ocala, Florida, reported to the *Auk* (April 1974) that she and a friend saw a pair of cardinals habitually feed on the blossoms of shrimp plants. Wible and her friend first noticed this practice when they saw a male cardinal eating blossoms that had fallen on the ground. The male then flew up into the dense foliage of the plants, where he was seen plucking the flowers and eating a portion of them before dropping what remained to the ground. Soon he was joined by a female cardinal, who followed his example. When they were finished, Wible examined the blossoms and determined that the birds had eaten only the small greenish white capsule at the base of the calyx, which was missing from the blossoms the birds had dropped on the ground. This capsule is sticky to the touch and sweet to the taste. So it would appear that hummingbirds are not the only avian species that visit plants for their nectar. At least in Florida, cardinals also enjoy this natural treat.

In a letter to Arthur Cleveland Bent, the Rev. J. J. Murray once noted a pair of cardinals that visited the holes made in a maple tree by sapsuckers. It was early in March, when the sap was running freely, and, according to Murray, the birds were drinking greedily.

In a paper on the food of grosbeaks, W. L. McAtee gives the results attained from the examination of nearly five hundred stomachs of Northern Cardinals. His examination showed that three-tenths of a cardinal's diet is animal and seven-tenths vegetable. Included in the animal part was a portion of a field mouse that one male cardinal had consumed.

Additionally, cardinals are easily attracted to mealworms, a welcome supplement, especially during nesting. The adult birds bring them to the nestlings. You may ask how a supply of mealworms can be obtained. You can raise them at home, or they may be purchased from bait or pet shops. If all else fails, ask the nearest biology teacher for a supply catalog from which they may be ordered.

Though cardinals are mainly seed eaters, they also eat a variety of insects that are considered harmful to crops. The pesky green caterpillars that defoliate oaks and descend to the ground on thin webs are sometimes caught by cardinals in typical flycatcher fashion. Other birds, like Yellow-rumped Warblers and

Cedar Waxwings, practice this type of food gathering, but they are notably winter visitors, rather than permanent residents like the cardinals.

Northern Cardinals eat more than fifty kinds of beetles, cicadas, dragonflies, leafhoppers, treehoppers, aphids, scale insects, ants, sawflies, termites, grasshoppers, crickets, caterpillars, codling moths, and cutworms. They also eat wood borers, fireflies, billbugs, and plant lice. This impressive array of insects on the cardinal's menu is enough to entitle the bird to the esteem of farmers and gardeners alike. Indeed, insects make up almost one-third of a cardinal's diet.

Like most insectivorous birds, cardinals love suet and suet mixes, too. Try this recipe that is a delight to cardinals as well as to many other kinds of birds that come to winter feeding stations, but remember it is recommended as a winter food only. In warm weather the oil from such a mixture can result in infection of feather follicles. A safe summer recipe appears on p. 55.

Recipe for Suet/Peanut Butter Mixture
(Winter Recipe)

1 cup of grease
1 cup of water
2 or 3 tablespoons of sugar (optional)
2 cups of cornmeal or oatmeal
½ cup crunchy peanut butter

The grease can be that which is melted out of suet scraps, or it can be waste fats from cooking, bacon grease, or lard. Heat the first four ingredients together until the mixture thickens. Remove from heat and add peanut butter. After cooling, place globs of this into holes drilled in a small log that can be hung in a tree. Make sure the log has a perch on it for the cardinals. A dowel pin can be used as a perch. Be prepared to fill the log often on cold days. Store the remaining mixture in the refrigerator.

Some authorities believe an increased interest in winter feeding has expanded the range of the Northern Cardinal.

Log feeder for suet and peanut butter mixture.
Drawing by Sam Osborne.

In addition to cardinals, a variety of other birds love this mixture, including chickadees, titmice, jays, woodpeckers, wrens, Ruby-crowned Kinglets, American Goldfinches, Purple Finches, Pine Siskins, and Yellow-rumped and Orange-crowned Warblers.

I first began feeding birds in my backyard in 1975. Since then, over forty species have come to the smorgasbord spread for them there. In addition, I have recorded well over one hundred species of birds sighted from our property, either feeding or flying overhead. Out of all those species, the cardinal remains our family favorite.

A few years after I started this feeding project my oldest son was visiting at home. He and I were sitting in the backyard watching a family of cardinals, and he commented, "Mom, your yard is virtually a bird sanctuary now, isn't it?" Up until then I had not thought of it as such; but, yes, it is. In order for this to happen in your yard, four basic ingredients are required: food, water, shelter, and a window. The first three ingredients are for the birds; the window is for you. A friend once told me, "What *I* can see is what *they* get." He saw no purpose in placing a bird feeder out of his line of vision. Neither do I.

Birds need water for drinking as well as for bathing to keep their plumage in tip-top condition both in summer and winter. Anything from an upside-down garbage can lid to an elaborate birdbath with a flowing fountain will do. Like small children, some birds, including cardinals, enjoy bathing in lawn sprinklers, and like watching children, watching cardinals can be quite entertaining.

Birds need shelter (or cover) for protection from weather and from predators and for a place to rest and raise their young. Existing plants, trees, shrubs, or homemade brush piles serve this purpose.

You need the window through which to view the scene now animated with birds going about the business of their daily lives. Through this window you may be privy to the most intimate of cardinal behavior that begins to unfold during this season of the year. Once the stage is set, up with the curtain and on with the show.

Shortly after Barbara Garland started feeding birds in her yard, she witnessed a small drama when she began to watch the behavior of a pair of cardinals. She first noticed the male because when he flew to a tree to perch he seemed unsteady and flopped around before gaining equilibrium. At first she thought he had an injured wing, but after the bird landed he seemed normal except that he sat very low on the limb and pumped his tail in un-cardinal-like fashion.

Finally, after several months of observing this behavior, Barbara discovered the reason for his unbalanced landing act. One day when he landed on the birdbath with his back to her, he leaned forward to get a drink. When he did, his right leg extended backward, and it was clearly apparent that the bird was missing his right foot.

Granted, this is not so unusual. A lot of birds meet with misfortune. The bizarre aspect of this story is that the male's mate was also minus her right foot. Of course, there is no way to know how or why both birds of this mated pair had the same handicap. Was it genetic? Was it accidental? No one knows. One can only speculate. Barbara observed the same two birds

Through your window you may view birds going about the business of their daily lives.

around her feeders for two years in a row, and they raised normal offspring through two breeding seasons. Had she not been feeding birds in her yard, she would have missed this avian drama.

Courtship: Visual and Vocal Displays

Not only is February the season of intensive winter feeding; it is also the season that initiates visual displays in which courtship and breeding accelerate and become highly visible right outside our windows. On a cold morning in late February, a flash of red catches my eye as I walk past the dining room window. I stop and grab the binoculars that I keep close by. A male cardinal, his feathers fluffed against the chill, comes into focus. He is on the ground beneath the feeder. He picks up a black oil sunflower seed in his bill, hops toward the hedge, and stops. I hear the familiar "*chink*" call note as he looks warily in all directions. He hops a few more inches and stops again. Then I hear an answering "*chink*" coming from somewhere inside the hedge. As I scan the shrub with my binoculars I see a female cardinal perched on a limb a short distance from the outer edge of the foliage. Her wings are quivering like those of a baby bird begging for food as she watches the male's every move.

After a moment he flies up into the hedge, utters a piping call, and lands on the sawed-off stub of a limb near the female. He still has the seed in his beak. Soon the two are face to face, and her wings are still aflutter. She opens her mouth and stands waiting. Methodically, the male rotates the seed in his thick bill, cracks it, extracts the nutmeat, and discards the shell. The female tilts her head to one side, and he transfers the tidbit from his bill to hers as gently as lovers exchanging a first kiss. This is a sign of pair bonding. It is like the box of candy or bouquet of flowers among humans. Mate feeding is one of the first visible steps in the breeding cycle of cardinals, and it is not unusual to see this behavior on or near your feeders.

True, only a few weeks earlier I may have seen a little aggressiveness on the part of the male cardinal when both were present in the feeding area. At that time the male made a threatening move toward the female as if attempting to drive her away. At such a time she either moved out of his way or ignored him entirely. It looked as if the honeymoon was over before it started. But such male aggression is typical behavior in mated pairs of cardinals at that time of year. However, once mate feeding begins, the two dine together peacefully throughout the breeding process.

Courtship feeding such as that described between the cardinals is not uncommon among other birds. It has been reported in some forty different families of birds. When you see this type of behavior at your feeder or at woodland edge, you know that courtship between the cardinals has officially begun. Can spring be far behind?

Courtship rituals among the more than nine thousand species of birds in the world range from elaborate to elemental. Cranes, storks, and herons are noted for their complex mating dances, which almost seem choreographed as both sexes come together to perform their graceful ballets. They spread their wings, jump up in the air, and then bow as they call out to one another.

Male Greater and Lesser prairie chickens dance and strut on a traditional breeding ground called a "lek" until a female takes notice and invites one of them to the sidelines for copulation. The Golden Eagle does a fluttering dance high in the sky that ends in a gigantic dive toward its lofty nest. Male terns prance around the shoreline with fish in their beaks or burst into ceremonial flights until a female acknowledges the "good provider" and allows copulation to occur and thus a pair bond to form. Western Grebes dance on the water in their courtship rituals. Mate feeding between the cardinals may not be as showy as some of these rituals, but all these displays, whether elaborate or simple, are means to an end—establishing the pair bond.

Many species of birds are polygamous; however, most are monogamous, at least for a single breeding season if not for life. Many (although not all) ornithologists believe that cardinals mate for life. In other words, a bonded pair of cardinals remains together not only for the breeding season, but for the rest of the year as well. If either mate dies, usually the remaining bird searches for and finds another mate.

How often have you seen at your feeder just one cardinal—a male or a female—in any given season? I daresay your answer is "not often." Usually, when you see one of the pair present, the other is not far away, and you hear their "*chink*" network of communication.

Some ornithologists believe that it is the individual birds' attachment to the nesting site, not their attachment to each other, that brings pairs together year after year. Most bird lovers prefer to believe it is the birds' devotion to each other. But that opinion is considered anthropomorphic and not scientific. Sometimes it is difficult not to be anthropomorphic, especially during what we consider the season of love.

Another sign that spring and breeding season are not far away is the heightened level of countersinging between the pair of cardinals. Often the male sings two or three phrases of a typical cardinal song and then suddenly stops. You may wonder, "Why doesn't he finish his song?" Then, in a few seconds, from somewhere in the distance, you hear the female answer. She matches his song, phrase for phrase, or finishes the song he started—a true Nelson Eddy/Jeanette MacDonald type of duet. This lovely antiphony can go on for hours, with variations in phrasing, and serves as another aid to strengthen their bond.

To me the antiphonal sound, linked with peace at the feeding station, is as welcome as an orchestral overture after a discordant warm-up. It is the signal that the cardinals really mean business. And then those pounds and pounds of black oil sunflower seeds I have provided through the long, cold winter begin to pay off.

For example, I may see a display that Donald and Lillian Stokes describe as the "lopsided-pose," in which one bird of the mated pair raises a wing and spreads the feathers fully, creating a lopsided effect. Or the bird may simply lean to one side without raising the wing. The feathers in the crest are

In an act of pair bonding the male extracts the nutmeat, discards the shell, and transfers the tidbit from his bill to hers.

One courtship ritual that may be described as the "lopsided pose" is usually performed within sight of the mate.

lowered, and the neck and body feathers are sleeked down. The bird rocks back and forth in a swaying fashion, raising first one foot and then the other. The bill is shut during this display, but the bird may utter "*chuck*" calls. The other bird, not more than a few feet away, suddenly joins in this little dance and mimics the first bird's actions. I know of no explanation about why this is done. It merely seems to be a part of the courtship ritual.

Another ceremony incorporates both the visual and the vocal aspects of behavior. It is called "song-flight." The male fluffs out all his breast feathers, raises his crest, sings while flying toward the female, and alights near her. Such flights have been noted ranging in distance from ten to one hundred feet. Occasionally the male directs this song-flight toward a trespassing female in the presence of his mated partner. When this happens the intruding female simply flies away from the displaying male.

Also, a "song-dance" display is entertaining to watch. Several components of the lopsided ritual are evident in this advertisement of sexual prowess, such as shifting the weight of the body from one side to the other; however, in this display the male may change from an erect, upright posture while singing to a bowing posture with bill pointed toward the ground. It is almost like a square-dance routine—"Honor your partner. Do-si-do."

In February and March, defending the territory becomes paramount in the life of the male cardinal. He goes to great lengths to ensure that his block of land is safe from all other intruding males of the species.

On a sunny February morning near Rockport, Texas, Barbara Garland and I stood right at the juncture of the territories of at least four male cardinals. We were surrounded by their territorial proclamations. Every few minutes, one of the males dared to cross over the invisible boundary of another male's territory. Then there ensued a chase reminiscent of the dogfights of World War II fighter planes. The incumbent male flew after the intruder at breakneck speed, dodging tree limbs with the agility of a swallow in flight. This activity continued until the interloper went back to his own high perch and resumed his territorial song.

Not only does the male cardinal chase away these interlopers, he has been known to attack a piece of red paper or other material or bump against his own reflection in hubcaps, car mirrors, or picture windows and sliding glass doors. This can be quite disruptive to the peaceful life of a homeowner. When the bird sees his image in the shiny surface, he assumes another cardinal is vying for his territory. Often residents are puzzled by this bizarre behavior and think they have a deranged cardinal on their hands when the bird repeatedly bangs his head against the reflection, as if shadowboxing, hour after hour. This relentless battle may persist for days. Occasionally, the female exhibits the same type of behavior. Sometimes it becomes necessary to cover shiny surfaces to restore peace and quiet to the homeowners, to say nothing of trying to keep the bird from harming itself in these near-suicidal attacks.

Another visual display used by the Northern Cardinal as a defense mechanism is described by the Stokeses as "head-forward" behavior. In a situation involving any type of aggression toward another bird, be it an intruding member of the same species or simply a different species jockeying for position at a feeder, the bird crouches with its body in a horizontal position. Its head is thrust forward with crest smoothly lowered, and its mouth may be opened or closed. This is supposed to seem threatening to the other bird.

I have seen this scenario many times at a small tray feeder outside my window. A House Sparrow, for instance, may be eating alone at the feeder, when suddenly a cardinal flies in and lands on the same feeder. When the cardinal goes into this act meant to frighten, with its head thrust forward toward the sparrow, the sparrow departs straightaway and does not return until the cardinal has finished feeding.

These are some of the types of cardinal behavior you may be privileged to observe through your own windows during February and March if you establish a bird sanctuary in your backyard. You provide the food, drink, and shelter, and the birds

In a display of mild aggression the bird lowers its crest and hunches forward.

provide the entertainment. When the stage is set and the curtains are drawn, all the elements that we have come to expect in entertainment are there—sex, violence, tenderness, love triangles, domestic strife, domestic tranquility—and the only charge is the cost of a few pounds of seeds.

Most birds nest in spring and summer . . . because all conditions are then most favorable: warmth, full foliage for hiding nests, abundance of food, long days for gathering it for their young.

—Alexander F. Skutch

Infancy, we say, is hedged about by many perils; but the infancy of birds is cradled and pillowed in peril.

—John Burroughs

April through July:
Nesting and Breeding Season

*B*iology professor Fred Gehlbach examined eight eastern and central North American suburban breeding bird censuses (Ohio, Ontario, Kansas, Massachusetts, New Jersey, North Carolina, Texas, Washington, D.C.) and found the Northern Cardinal to be the seventh most widespread and frequent nesting species. It fell behind the European Starling, American Robin, House Sparrow, Blue Jay, Common Grackle, and Song Sparrow. In his study plot in Columbus, Ohio, however, the cardinal ranked sixth, and at Waco, Texas, third.

In the Deep South, nesting sometimes begins in February, but in most parts of the country, Northern Cardinals begin building their nests in early April. In the more northern areas of the cardinal's range, nesting may begin considerably later. Cardinals, like most other songbirds, build complex cupped nests in which to lay their eggs and raise their young, and they use a variety of places and a diversity of vegetation.

From the human's point of view, the name of the avian game seems to be concealment since nests are fairly hard to locate. The fact is, we don't *know* whether birds deliberately set out to place their nests where they will be hidden or not.

How do cardinals go about deciding where to build their nests? The process of site selection is almost always basically the same, step by step, and may be illustrated by a scenario that took place several times over a period of two years only inches from the window of my study. The first time I observed the action in the nandina bush, a male cardinal hopped slowly and deliberately from one branch to another, saying *"chink"* from time to time as he seemed to examine the configuration of the branches. He lingered awhile in the section next to the window screen then hopped to the outer edge of the bush and looked toward the neighbor's house where I saw the female cardinal perched in a shrub watching him. After repeating *"chink"* a few more times, he sang a brief song and flew over to her.

Soon the female came to the bush to look around. She explored the same branches the male had examined, and he joined her there. She crouched in one spot for a few minutes as if sitting on a nest. The male came to her side and sat very close to her. "*Chinks*" flew back and forth between them faster than a tennis ball at Wimbledon. I began to suspect they were looking for a nesting site.

Advantages and disadvantages of using this particular bush were clearly apparent to me, and probably to the birds as well. At first it seemed an almost ideal location as far as shelter was concerned. Here, with thick overhanging leaves, they would be protected from sun and rain. Moreover, the bush was only fifteen yards from the sunflower feeder in my backyard, which would provide a convenient food supply.

The major disadvantage that I recognized was the large cat that had raided the mockingbird's nest one week before in a holly bush just six feet away. Of course, I have no idea whether the cat was a factor, but, for whatever reasons, the pair did not begin transporting nest materials to the bush as I had hoped they would.

Nevertheless, so goes the selective process of cardinals looking for the best location for a nest. The intervals of searching increase in length daily as the nest-building drive matures. The pair may spend several days going from site to site within their territory, searching, as these two did outside my window, until they find a satisfactory location. Over the next several days, the scenario was repeated in the same bush at least three times by the birds that year. And the same thing happened the following spring. Each time my expectations rose to a higher level; each time there was a disappointing ending after a promising buildup. I suppose it was too much to ask for a pair of cardinals to nest right outside my window while this book was in preparation.

Cardinals nest in a surprising assortment of vegetation and places. Despite the intensity of the nest site search, cardinals make their homes sometimes in precarious places with life-and-death consequences. When Barbara Garland was searching for nests to photograph for this book, she at first found six. The first, in a suburban area, was in a mock orange tree 5½ feet from the ground. After the eggs had been hatched only a few days, a neighborhood dog destroyed both nest and nestlings.

The second was in a huge blackjack oak tree with long spreading limbs that almost touched the ground. This nest, at the end of one of the low-hanging limbs, was only four feet off the ground. One morning the homeowners at this rural location watched in horror as a snake ate all four eggs that were in the nest. Cardinals are known for this seemingly careless, close-to-the-ground nest site selection, which seems odd to us after such a long search.

A boxwood hedge provided concealment for the third nest Barbara found. It was located next to a friend's house and about six feet from the ground. After sitting on two eggs for a few days, the female cardinal inexplicably abandoned the nest.

Barbara was beginning to think she would never find a successful nest. However, this type of destruction and disruption is really not unusual. Gehlbach's notes reveal that in his suburban study area long-term nesting success was 39 percent. That means a little more than one of every three nesting attempts was successful. In a rural study plot, he found success at 17 percent—less than one nest in five. Gehlbach concluded that these differences are statistically significant and in keeping with what is known about urban versus rural populations of a species in a particular geographic area—namely, the urban population is more successful, largely because of decreased predation.

Just when Barbara thought all was lost, a friend called and told her about a cardinal nest located in a waxleaf ligustrum adjacent to her home. The female cardinal on this nest succeeded in raising three young.

The fifth nest was in a topiary hedge. From a clutch of four eggs, only one nestling survived to leave the nest. The sixth nest was found barely clinging to the stalks of some dead bamboo shoots. Surprisingly, three babies fledged from this precarious site.

A nest in Toronto was found only two or three feet from one of the busiest walkways in High Park. Hundreds of people daily passed within arm's reach of the cardinal's nest, which was situated three feet from the ground in an Austrian pine. Another nest was found in a vine growing on the side wall of someone's back porch directly under the kitchen window and three or four feet from a door through which people passed in and out all day.

My son's family witnessed a cardinal family thrive nestled in a hanging basket of boxwood fern inside a covered patio that was enclosed on three sides. The parent birds flew through the open end of the patio to attend their nesting duties. The next spring, after my son had placed screenwire across the open end of the patio, he saw a female cardinal hitting against the screen. Because the hanging basket was still in the same place, the family wondered if the same bird was attempting to nest there again.

I once found a cardinal building her nest in a Virginia creeper vine that clings to the screen on one of my bedroom windows. Arthur Cleveland Bent reports a nest built in a small bush inside a greenhouse connected to a flower shop in the center of a city. The birds gained entrance through a broken window pane that the owner obligingly put off repairing until after the young had fledged.

My friend Floyce Moon, a retired school teacher, told me of a cardinal pair who built their nest in a pyracantha bush about three feet outside one of her classroom windows. When her students were at the reading table they had ringside seats to all the activities, including nest building, incubation of the eggs, and feeding of the young. One Friday the nestlings began to hop onto the edge of the nest, and by Monday morning the nest was empty. When the first-graders arrived at school that morning, they were very disappointed that they had missed seeing the fledglings when they left the nest. But their disappointment abated later that day when they saw the whole cardinal family touring the area. It appeared that the young birds were being given a crash course on survival for the next several days. My friend knew the experience made a lasting impression on her students, because at the close of the school year the children wrote notes about what they had liked best about first grade. Nearly all of them named "the redbirds."

In 1944 Amelia R. Laskey studied 103 cardinal nests near Nashville, Tennessee. She reported: "As nest sites, cardinals choose young evergreens of many varieties; privet hedges; many species of vines, including rose and honeysuckle; shrubbery; and saplings of hackberry, elm, hawthorn, and locust." She said one cardinal built a nest on a platform of twigs that she personally placed in a privet shrub where the birds had tried unsuccessfully to anchor nesting materials.

In the Everglades, cardinals may nest in bushes along the banks of the canals. In other parts of Florida, nests are found in palmetto or oak bushes, in small orange trees, in clumps of vines, or saddled on the limbs of mango trees. In Arizona and other areas in the Southwest you may see cardinals nesting in mesquite trees. In Mississippi they are found in orchards and the thickest of canebrakes among a variety of other places. In Central Texas one may find them in dense shrubs, especially coralberry and deciduous holly, in vine tangles of greenbrier, and in shrubby eastern red cedar trees.

In the southern Alleghenies cardinals prefer the edges of brooks, rocky slopes, and dense ravines where azaleas, rhododendrons, mountain laurels, and many other sweet-scented shrubs form dense and extensive thickets. In southwestern Missouri, Henry Nehrling found cardinals nesting in snowberry, wild rose, and gooseberry bushes. In southern Louisiana he found them in the undergrowth on the edges of cypress swamps. All over the South he discovered numerous nests in the beautiful dense hedges of Cherokee rose.

Cardinals rarely build their nests in the open. Surprisingly, Gehlbach found a successful one in a lone four-foot shrub by a window, bordered on the outside by a concrete driveway. Laskey reports a cardinal nest on the ledge of a lattice fence between pieces of poultry wire with nothing for concealment. Another rare nest site was on a feeding shelf outside a second-story window. One of the most bizarre cardinal nest sites was in a woven-wire sparrow trap on a beam fifteen feet above the floor in an outbuilding. The cardinals successfully nested there in two different seasons.

This wide variety makes it quite evident that cardinals are not averse to living near habitations and they show no marked preference as to the kind of vegetation in which they nest, apart from a strong affinity for dense understory.

From all these descriptions it seems that cardinals prefer to nest at fairly low levels. Their nests are generally placed between three and twenty feet from the ground, more often below ten feet. A nest placed more than twenty feet high is rare but not unheard of. On a river bank in a flooded area, Barbara found a cardinal nest thirty feet high in an elm tree.

Nest sizes among birds generally vary according to the size of the bird. Not surprisingly, hummingbirds make the smallest ones. The Ruby-throated Hummingbird's nest is no bigger than a demitasse—about an inch deep and an inch across. The largest tree nests of birds in North America are those of the Bald Eagle. One measured 20 feet deep and 9½ feet across. A cardinal's nest would seem dwarfed if placed alongside one of such gargantuan proportions. The cupped nest of the Northern Cardinal has a depth of 1⅝ inches, a height of 3¼ inches, and an outside diameter of 5⅜ inches.

There is wide diversity in the kinds of nests constructed by different birds—from the floating nests of grebes and coots to the large platforms of sticks used by Ospreys and the simple scrapes on bare ground used by gulls, terns, and many other shorebirds. Most of the songbirds, including cardinals, build open cuplike nests.

In some species of the world's birds, both male and female assist in assembling the nest. In other species, only one partner participates. In shrikes the male builds the nest alone. In hummingbirds, the male never even sees the nest. In the case of the Northern Cardinal, the female does most of the construction herself, but the male is never far away. Many times he helps his mate in gathering building materials and occasionally assists in their placement.

Once the site selection is made, a pair of cardinals will cruise their territory searching for all the "right stuff" that goes into the nest. The female usually leads as the two fly across an open area. One or both may have nesting materials in their beaks. A good way to find a cardinal nest is to follow the female when you see her repeatedly going into the same thicket or shrub, but be very careful not to disturb. Human curiosity is often due cause for a bird to build a new nest in a different location. So, if you must watch, do so from a safe distance.

Just what is the "right stuff" for cardinal nests? Naturally, it depends on the part of the country in which you look. In some localities you might find grasses and fine rootlets, old leaves, horse hair, pine needles, twigs, grapevine bark, weed stems, rags, forb stalks, strips of paper, and other debris. In a nest found in a ravine in Central Texas, the major component was red cedar bark strips. A cardinal nest in the swamps of Louisiana may be composed almost entirely of Spanish moss and grasses and decorated with a snake skin around the rim. A nest in Tamaulipas, Mexico, may contain a large amount of goat's hair in the lining.

A third-grader once called me and said her class was studying birds, and her assignment was to build a nest like a cardinal's. She asked my advice on how to go about it. Even though I had watched cardinals building a nest I was hard put to give her an answer. An old French proverb says that humans can do everything except build a bird's nest. If you've ever watched the nest building process, undoubtedly you will agree. I once observed a hummingbird daily from the time it attached a small platform on a down-sloping branch of a pecan tree until it decorated the outside of the finished structure with tiny bits of lichen which it stuck in place with its own saliva. I've never seen a human-made form to equal it.

It is amazing to think that the only tools most birds use are their bills and feet, and yet they are able to weave complex structures that stand up to the worst of adversities and look like works of art. Doubtless, few humans are capable of building a house using only their mouths and feet as tools. Since a bird's bill is primarily adapted for eating or food gathering, one might suppose the avian architect has difficulty in using the same tool for building purposes. Most birds, though, seem adept at making this adjustment, and the cardinal is no exception. It uses its short, stout seed-cracking bill quite efficiently when it comes time to fetch, place, and organize the materials it chooses for its nest. Likewise, its feet, used primarily for perching, skillfully come into play for pushing, lifting, and arranging the building supplies required for the inside layer of the cuplike receptacle.

The actual process of building the nest is roughly divided into three steps: preparing the site or support, constructing the floor and sides, and lining the nest. A cardinal nest has four distinct layers. The first layer, or foundation, is a platform of stiff weed stems or small sticks that the female carefully places in the selected site. Incidentally, the bird who builds in a bush must know just what configuration of branches is needed to provide adequate support for the nest. That is one reason it takes considerable time to find just the right place. No doubt this knowledge is gained through trial and error.

The second layer is of softer, more pliable materials, such as old leaves, strips of various kinds of bark, pieces of paper, or grass. This layer forms the outside walls of the cupped nest. Some cardinal nests I have examined are really sloppy, having loose strands of paper hanging out all around them.

The third layer consists of finer weeds and grasses and trailing vines. During the process of completing this layer, the female sits in the middle of the cup that is taking shape, and pulls long slender pieces of plant fiber, one at a time with her bill, inward over the rim. She tucks each of these into the wall under her breast or alongside her body. She squats inside the nest and presses—with her head, her feet, her wings, her tail, or her whole body—against the rim of the cup. Rotating her body, she repeats these actions each time she brings new materials to the site, thus forming a round nest. Next she loops a similar bit of fiber around a supporting branch and secures the end of it inside the wall of the nest. She repeats this step until the structure is securely tied to several supporting branches.

The fourth, and final, layer is the softest. It is the lining where she lays the eggs—the equivalent of the receiving blanket in the nursery where the young will be nurtured. It contains fine rootlets, pine needles, horse hair, goat hair, dog hair, human hair, or Spanish moss—anything soft that is available. When forming this layer, she nestles as low as she can inside the concavity and squirms about until the fit is perfect and there is plenty of room underneath her for the eggs.

During the nesting season, it is fun to place strands of yarn or clumps of hair in a bush or tree and watch for the cardinals and other birds to find them. It usually does not take the birds long to discover the treasures.

Even with all the complicated weaving, squirming, poking, and pushing, the female cardinal still ends up with a rather frail and loose structure. If you could examine a nest closely, you might wonder how the parent birds ever succeed in bringing up young in such a receptacle.

The length of time required to build a nest varies with weather conditions, availability of supplies, and with the species. Some birds spend months on nest construction. Greater Thornbirds of Paraguay may work all winter on their huge stick nests. Bushtits take up to fifty days on their foot long hanging pocket nests. The Ruby-throated Hummingbird I watched spent five days completing hers, and I do not know how long she had been working before I discovered it. A Golden Eagle may take up to two months, and Northern Orioles ten to twelve days.

Recorded lengths of time for cardinals to complete their nests range from three to nine days. Thus cardinals are on the lower end of the scale of time spent on construction. Moreover, birds do not work constantly, all day long, nor every day. They usually work for a few hours early in the morning and a few hours late in the evening until the nest is complete. And, just as construction crews sometimes have to postpone outside work if inclement weather occurs, so may cardinals delay their work for a day or two until conditions improve.

Birds expend a tremendous amount of energy in the process of nest building. Barn Swallows make more than 1,200 trips to collect the mud needed for only one nest. A Black-throated Oriole's nest in Mexico was found to contain 3,387 separate pieces of grass and plant fibers. I don't know how many items go into a cardinal nest, but on a museum specimen of a hummingbird's nest I counted over 250 bits of lichen, and that was just the decoration on the outside walls. In a House Sparrow's nest near Chapel Hill, North Carolina, John K. Terres reported 1,282 items. The list included mostly grasses and some strips of grapevine bark, but it also included part of an envelope postmarked "New York 17" and, appropriately, a piece of a letter bearing the typed words "difficult struggle."

In most birds, copulation occurs intermittently during the period between pair bonding and egg laying and sometimes continues through incubation and care of the young. This is true especially in those birds that raise more than one brood as do the cardinals. Although in most cases the male is the aggressor, the female often invites coition by song, call note, a particular posture, or a provocative display. The song of the female cardinal seems to be one of the strongest stimuli for the male.

Donald and Lillian Stokes report that it is not all that common to observe cardinals in the act of mating. Robert E. Lemon found this to be true in his study of cardinals in Ontario: "Actual copulation was noted only a few times in the wild and then only from some distance."

While Barbara Garland was photographing cardinals for this book she observed cardinals mating on three different occasions. She said the first time she saw a pair mate, the female was perched perpendicular to a branch with her wings lowered and quivering while she awaited the male's approach. When he appeared his crest was erect and he looked really alert. When he got close to the female, she crouched down with her beak and tail pointed upward and her breast feathers fluffed. She spread her tail to one side so that her vent (cloacal opening) was exposed. The male sidled down the limb to her, mounted her back, touched her vent with his, and thus transmitted the sperm from his body to hers. It was over almost in the blinking of an eye—too fast for Barbara even to focus the camera.

Barbara's second observation of coition between cardinals was the pair who each had only one foot. Not surprisingly, these two mated on the ground, solving their balancing problems. The third time she observed mating, the cardinals had just finished feeding nestlings. This time coition occurred on the rim of the nest, and although Barbara was ready for the action with her camera, her flash failed to perform.

The Values of Summer Feeding throughout Egg Laying, Incubation, and Care of the Young

The interval between completion of the nest and laying of the first egg varies among species as well as among individual birds. With cardinals egg laying usually begins up to six days after the nest is finished. After expending so much effort on gathering building supplies and actually constructing the nest, most female birds take time to rest and renew their energy before laying their eggs. This is one reason it is important to continue feeding the birds through the breeding season even though natural foods are in abundance at this time. Birds will readily take the supplemental nourishment you provide for their myriad calorie-consuming activities connected with breeding. Additionally, an accessible food supply may encourage the birds to nest in your garden.

The following are some suggestions of items you can easily provide for this critical time in the life of your favorite redbirds:

1. Finely crushed eggshells provide females with added calcium vital to the development of eggs in their own bodies. These can be offered in the feeder right along with sunflower seeds.

2. A peanut butter mixture for summertime feeding to take the place of the suet mixture mentioned earlier for the winter months is designed not to become rancid in summer heat. Mix together in a bowl: one part peanut butter, four parts cornmeal, one part flour, and one part vegetable shortening. No cooking is necessary. This can be offered in the same sort of feeder as earlier suggested for the suet mix—a hanging log with perches. Store any excess in the refrigerator.

3. Mealworms are another source of vital nutrients to offer at summer feeding stations. They are readily eaten by cardinals, and the adults often feed them to their young. As previously suggested, buy mealworms at a bait shop or pet store, or ask a biology teacher for a supply catalog.

After a few days of rest, it is time for the female to get on with her task of egg laying. Once the male's sperm cells enter her body they swim to the upper end of the oviduct, where one fertilizes the ovum (yolk) before the shell forms around it. Thus begins the development of an embryo.

The ovum goes through several stages as it passes through the reproductive tract of the female. At one stage the egg white (albumen) forms. Next the inner and outer shell membranes are formed. Then the ovum moves into the uterus, where it remains for a little over twenty hours. At this stage, during the last five hours before the egg is actually laid, the hard outer shell is formed and colored with pigments.

There is an almost infinite variety in the colors and markings of bird eggs. Even within a species, eggs can be remarkably diverse, sometimes making it difficult for a novice to determine the kind of bird that laid them. Some birds produce eggs that are uniformly colored. For example, a woodpecker's eggs are pure white, highly glossy, and look like the finest of translucent porcelains. Robins' and bluebirds' eggs are light blue. The Great Tinamou of the tropical American forests lays eggs that are intense turquoise blue with a high gloss.

Most birds, however, produce eggs with some combination of ground color and various markings. These markings may be in the form of blotches, scrawls, streaks, marbling, or speckles. Northern Cardinal eggs follow this pattern. Usually the largest concentration of color forms a wreath around the large end of the egg, since it passes first through the major supply of pigments from the cellular walls of the bird's birth canal.

Egg size varies among species almost as much as color. The egg of one of the smallest hummingbirds is one-half inch in length by one-quarter inch in thickness and weighs about 0.3 grams. An ostrich egg, on the opposite end of the scale, is six inches by five inches and weighs 1,600 grams. Between these two extremes we find the cardinal's egg, which is about one inch long and weighs around 8.6 grams. Thus the ostrich egg weighs 5,333 times as much as the hummer's and 186 times as much as the cardinal's.

Most songbirds lay their eggs very early in the morning. When the time is right for the female cardinal, she enters the nest before daylight or the evening before. Once the egg is complete inside her body, it passes quickly through the muscular cloaca. During the next stage, the bird may rise from time to time and look beneath her to see if anything is happening. After one to three minutes of bearing down, the female expels her first egg, blunt end first, through the cloaca.

Approximately twenty-four hours later the entire process is repeated and a second egg appears in the nest. This goes on daily until the clutch is complete. A clutch is the total number of eggs laid in an uninterrupted series, for a single nesting, by one female. This is not to be confused with the total number of eggs found in a given nest, as various circumstances may affect the final count. For example, predators may remove or eat some of the eggs, or other birds may lay their eggs in the cardinal's nest, as we shall see later.

Occasionally two females of the same species lay their eggs in one nest and then share incubation duties. Oscar Hawksley and Alvah P. McCormack found a nest on which two female cardinals were actually incubating at the same time facing in opposite directions. In Topeka, Kansas, a partially albino cardinal and a normally colored one shared a nest. Together they incubated five eggs that were apparently the product of both females fertilized by one male—an exception to monogamy. When the young hatched, all three adult birds shared in feeding the five nestlings.

There is at least one instance on record when joint nesting efforts were undertaken by birds of two genera. Mr. and Mrs. George Swinford, of Erlanger, Kentucky, were surprised to find pairs of Northern Cardinals and American Robins sharing the same nest in a forsythia bush beside their porch. Karl Maslowski, a professional nature photographer and writer, was called upon to document the unusual occurrence on film. He reported that the nest construction was definitely a community effort, because the bottom half was typical of most cardinal nests and the top half was a robin's stick-and-mud bowl lined with grass.

When Maslowski first examined the nest he found four robin nestlings, two cardinals, and one unhatched cardinal egg. He observed that the females of both species shared brooding responsibilities, and both males assisted in feeding the babies. He reported that when the nestlings were young, the adult birds cross-fed all of them, but when they were about one week old, the parents began to feed only their own offspring. All the young of this unusual nesting co-op were raised to fledgling stage.

For now, consider normal the cardinal's clutch of two to five eggs, three to four being most common. The eggs are typically oval—sometimes long-oval, sometimes short-oval—with an overall measurement of 25.3 millimeters by 18.2 millimeters (about one inch long), and they weigh about 8.6 grams. They are smooth and semiglossy with a background color of white or slightly greenish, speckled and spotted in various degrees with small blotches of brown and reddish brown to pale purple and gray. As a rule, the heaviest spotting is concentrated on the larger end of the egg. However, sometimes the egg's surface is so heavily blotched that the background color is almost totally obscured.

Shortly after the egg is laid, a small air pocket forms at the large end between the two membranes that rest against the inside wall of the shell. As the embryo develops, water evaporates from the egg and the air chamber grows larger. A few hours before hatching, the embryo shifts positions and the head and bill come in contact with the membrane, which is then pierced. The baby cardinal begins to breathe this unique oxygen supply in preparation for its debut into the outside world.

Among cardinals, incubation at full intensity doesn't begin until after the last egg of the clutch is laid. Incubation is the act of a parent bird sitting on its eggs and applying body heat. Maintaining a constant temperature is vital to the rapid development of the embryos and the ultimate hatching of the chicks.

In order to accomplish this transfer of heat from the incubating bird to the eggs, most songbirds develop what is called an incubation patch—a small area on the abdomen from which the down feathers are dropped a few days before the eggs are to be laid. The blood vessels in this exposed area become enlarged and increase in number so that the skin thickens and becomes swollen. This heavy concentration of blood vessels near the surface provides a constant source of heat, roughly 104 degrees Fahrenheit. This special patch lasts for the duration of the breeding season whether only one brood or three to four are raised. The feathers on the abdomen are replaced during the fall molt, but until then, the incubating and brooding bird has a built-in heating pad.

When the female cardinal enters the nest to begin incubation, she carefully wiggles her body around until she can best cover the eggs. She fluffs her breast feathers so that the incubation patch is exposed and settles down on the eggs. Periodically she raises herself, turns the eggs with her bill, and then gently settles again in the nest, possibly facing in another direction.

During the application of this special heating pad, the embryo inside the tiny eggshell undergoes dramatic changes. A time-lapse photography sequence of what is occurring inside an egg would show that first the number of cells increases. When large enough numbers have formed, one of the most miraculous processes of life begins. Groups of cells move about and rearrange themselves, and through ensuing days the head, eyes, heart, and blood vessels start to form. In a surprisingly short time, a baby bird takes shape inside its protective covering of porous shell, which allows the transfer of oxygen and gaseous waste. While all this is happening, the yolk inside provides nutrition vital to the life of a healthy nestling, since there is no umbilical cord linking the embryo to its mother.

Generally speaking, in those species in which the sexes are outwardly alike, the male and female share equally in incubation of the eggs. The Killdeer is a familiar example of this pattern. Among phalaropes the male takes full responsibility for incubation and care of the young. However, with most passerines (songbirds) it is usually the duller-colored female, as in cardinals, that plays the major role in incubation. Supposedly, her dull color provides camouflage that protects her and the nestlings from detection by predators; but occasionally the crimson male cardinal will relieve his mate of these duties for short periods of time.

During the days the eggs are being incubated, the female seldom leaves the nest for long periods. Naturally she has to devote some time to her own health with short forays for feeding,

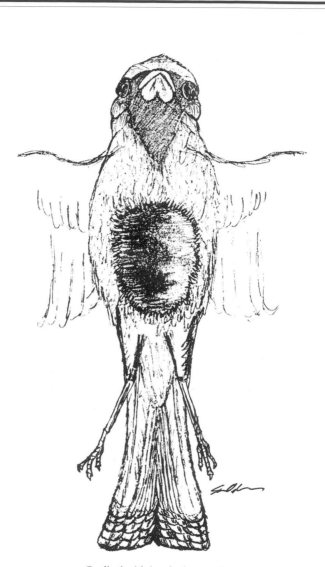

Cardinal with incubation patch.
Drawing by Sam Osborne.

bathing, and preening, but these jaunts are never lengthy. Throughout this critical time the male is very attentive to the female. He often sings near the nest, and once in awhile the female is heard answering his song with a soft one of her own from the nest. Or he may warn her with alarm notes if danger is near. Several times a day he brings food and feeds her in the same fashion as during their courtship period. This not only helps keep up her strength for the long days and hours of sitting; it also helps to strengthen the birds' attachment to each other. Often these visits end in coition, resulting in another brood.

Departure from and return to the nest by both birds of the pair follow the same pattern. When leaving the slightly elevated nest, the bird departs quickly in a downward direction and flies away at a low level to take advantage of the dense understory that usually surrounds the nest site. The procedure is reversed for the return to the nest. This extra caution is yet another deterrent to predators.

The time involved in incubation varies greatly among the species. Generally, those that produce well-developed (precocial) chicks take longer to incubate, and those with helpless (altricial) nestlings take a shorter time. Experts have found no incubation period shorter than eleven days. The Brown-headed Cowbird hatches after eleven days of incubation, which is definitely to the cowbird's advantage as we shall see later.

The Northern Cardinal's incubation period is usually twelve to thirteen days. When the baby bird is almost ready to hatch, it develops a strong "hatching muscle" and an egg tooth—a short, pointed calcareous structure on the tip of the upper half of its bill. Toward the end of the twelve to thirteen days, the fully developed embryo, with the help of its hatching muscle, rubs and scrapes its egg tooth against the walls of the shell, which have weakened because of loss of mineral substances that have dissolved out of the shell. The scraping continues until a small star-shaped puncture appears. This process is called *pipping*. During the next several hours the embryo pushes with its head and feet, alternately struggling and resting, until the cracks radiate around the larger end of the egg. When the cracks have weakened the shell sufficiently, the nestling works its way out, and a new life finds itself in daylight. The cardinal parents then either eat the eggshells or carry them some distance away from the nest to prevent betraying the nest's location to predators.

The first calls that baby cardinals make are faint sounds given at the time of hatching. By the time they leave the nest, nine to eleven days later, they give a variety of food-begging calls, which are slurred up or down.

One could hardly describe the newly hatched cardinal as "cute." It is an ungainly bundle of skin and bones—thin pink skin tightly drawn over a tiny skeleton and sparsely covered with mouse-gray natal down. It has bulging eyes covered with dark lids, a wobbly head, a swollen abdomen grotesquely disproportionate to the rest of its body, short undeveloped legs and wings, a large gaping mouth lined with bright red to make an easy target when being fed, and yellowish-white flanges (projecting folds of skin) outlining the red chasm that seems a bottomless pit. This is indeed a sight that only a mother bird could love. Within a week after hatching, the nestling's egg tooth gradually disappears without apparently falling off.

All birds are altricial or precocial at hatching. *Altricial* comes from the Latin word meaning "nurse." Helpless altricial youngsters require as much care as a human infant, and some believe that altricials are born prematurely. *Precocial,* the opposite of *altricial,* stems from the Latin word *Praecox,* "to ripen beforehand." The young chicks are able to move about shortly after hatching and require little or no parental care. They are born with their eyes wide open and are covered in down, a semblance of adult plumage. They leave the nest as soon as they are dry. Cardinals are altricial and thus require immediate care from their parents.

For awhile, cardinal nestlings are cold-blooded and unable to regulate their body temperature on their own. Since no bird has perfected a method for warming its young other than with its own body, the brooding parent must continue behavior similar to incubation and provide the necessary heat. Here again, that built-in heating pad comes in handy. Should the parent have to leave the nest for an extended period, the nestling's temperature drops or rises to the level of the surrounding air. In most cases this is not lethal unless the temperature is excessively low or excessively high. Excessive heat tends to be more of a threat to the life of a nestling than is cold. The brood-

Once the nest site is selected, the cardinals cruise their territory in search of "all the right stuff."

ing parent protects the young from sun and rain by covering the entire nest with outstretched wings like an umbrella. At about midpoint in nest life, the nestling attains body temperature control and no longer has to be brooded by the parent.

The newly hatched cardinal sprawls in the nest, too weak to hold up its head. It rests on its abdomen, its head slightly under its breast and its legs thrust forward. Early activities consist mainly of feeding, defecating, and sleeping. For a few hours after breaking out of the shell, the bird receives nourishment from the egg yolk which it absorbed in its stomach shortly before hatching. When that supply is depleted, the nestling lifts its wobbly head straight up, opens its mouth in a wide gape, and starts begging for food. The begging actions of the young, their yellowish flanges, and their bright red mouth lining all provide stimuli for the adult birds to begin feeding.

The next few days are frantically busy for both parents as they work to fill the gaping mouths of their three or four fast-growing, hungry nestlings. At a cardinal nest reported by A. C. Bent, over a period of 6½ hours the two young were fed 178 times, an average of 89 times each. The longest interval he noted between feeding visits was thirty-five minutes, and the shortest was two minutes.

The nestling's main diet for the first few days of life consists of insects—moths, bugs, larvae of various kinds, and green caterpillars and then later grasshoppers and beetles. W. L. McAtee noted that 94.75 percent of their food was found to be animal matter and 5.25 percent vegetable. The proportions of the principal food items of the nestlings he studied were as follows: cicadas, 17.25 percent; grasshoppers, 20 percent; caterpillars, 21.25 percent; and beetles, 23.25 percent. The vegetable matter consisted of corn, rice, kafir corn, oats, and wheat, all of which made up only 8.73 percent of the total food, and much of this was waste grain. He also listed thirty-three species of wild fruits that are occasionally fed to nestlings. The parents collect the food, return to the nest, turn their heads sideways, poke their beaks into the gullets of the nestlings to stimulate the swallowing reflex, and finally regurgitate the food deep into the young birds' throats.

The urge to feed is a very strong instinct in birds, sometimes even in those that are just beginning to nest. For example, some parent birds have been observed attempting to give food to the eggs. Once a young cardinal was placed in the nest of a Bell's Vireo just after the last egg of its clutch was laid. The vireo immediately began feeding the baby cardinal.

Sometimes the urge to feed transcends species and even class boundaries. A Northern Cardinal was observed in Shelby, North Carolina, feeding a group of goldfish in a pond. Perhaps the cardinal had lost its brood to predators, and when it went to the pond to drink, it saw the gaping mouths of the goldfish and couldn't resist the urge to feed them. For several days the cardinal expertly delivered mouthful after mouthful of worms to the hungry fish.

One might suppose that the parents feed their young by turns in rotation, but this is not the case. The hungriest gets fed first and continues to be fed until it is satisfied, then the next hungriest, and so on until all are fed. It seems to be a contest: whichever nestling raises its head the highest with its mouth wide open is first to be fed. When that nestling has had enough it ceases to swallow the food placed in its throat. The parent then lifts the unswallowed food from that nestling's throat and places it in the next highest open beak it sees. Alexander Skutch found that small songbirds are fed an average of four to twelve meals per hour per nestling. If those numbers hold true for a cardinal brood of four, the parents might make up to forty-eight trips per hour to feed their young. For nearly all species, the rate of feeding increases the longer the young are in the nest.

With that kind of service from attentive parents, the nestlings soon take on a growing spurt that is unequaled in the world of mammals. At the time of hatching, the weight of most passerine nestlings is equal to about two-thirds the weight of the fresh egg, or 6 to 8 percent of the weight of the adult female. When they are ready to leave the nest, at nine to eleven days of age, they weigh about 70 to 80 percent of the weight of the female parent.

In her study of Song Sparrows, Margaret Morse Nice notes

Both parents work diligently to feed their hungry nestlings.

that the first four days of nest life are characterized by rapid growth, the start of feather development, the food response, and defecation. This serves as a guide to the development of young cardinals as well. Days five and six are days of rapid weight gain, the establishment of temperature control, and a virtual explosion of feathers. Blue-sheathed feathers erupt as if in the hands of a magician. First they sprout as spiky quills; then they quickly grow and expand until the body is well covered. Sometime during these two days the nestling opens its eyes and begins standing, stretching its legs, and conducting rudimentary preening activities.

On days seven, eight, and nine, motor skill development is even more rapid. The nestlings begin to stretch and fan their wings, and they flutter them when begging for food. By the time the young leave the nest, they have lost their natal down and are covered by juvenal plumage. They are now fledglings.

In addition to feeding the young to spur their rapid growth, parent birds must keep the nest sanitary. Adult birds carry something away from the nest after almost every feeding episode. This is the fecal sac—a tough mucous membrane enclosing the feces of young nestlings. In cardinals this sac resembles a miniature disposable diaper. The high content of uric acid makes it white, and it looks like a small package neatly wrapped in white plastic.

Since the digestive tract of a nestling is far from perfect, each episode of feeding stimulates defecation. Usually the parent that brings food to the young waits on the side of the nest while the baby digests its food. After the nestling eats, it falls forward in the nest, exposes its vent, and defecates. The parent then reaches into the nest with its bill and removes the fecal sac, sometimes lifting it directly from the vent. Cardinal parents have been observed to eat the sac for four or five days after the nestlings hatch. This conservation measure makes use of the undigested food. Beginning about the fifth or sixth day the parents fly away from the nest before disposing of the sac so as not to reveal the nest's location to predators.

Defending the young in the nest from predators is another activity that consumes time and energy of the parent birds.

Cardinals have numerous enemies—raccoons, snakes, rats, cats, dogs, and, of course, other birds, such as hawks, crows, and owls.

Small birds have been observed dive-bombing cats and dogs and even people who came too close to their nests or young. Mockingbirds and Blue Jays are notorious for this behavior. During the nesting season I often receive phone calls from nervous homeowners who say they are being attacked by an angry bird every time they try to leave their homes. I explain to them that the bird is simply trying to defend its young from harm.

I also get calls from people asking the same question time and time again: "When a baby bird falls from a nest, if I pick it up and put it back, will the parents have anything more to do with the baby?" The answer is, "Yes, they will." An old wives' tale promotes the belief that once human hands touch a nestling or an egg, the parent birds will no longer care for that bird or egg. This is not true. It is just a myth. The human scent will not curtail the parents' responsibilities at the nest. What it may do, however, is attract predators to the nest. The lesson here is to think twice before you try to give human assistance in such an instance. Infancy of birds is, indeed, "cradled and pillowed in peril" from many quarters.

The Fledgling

Birds face many adversities while their young are still in the nest. It is a wonder that any survive to become fledglings, but survive they do. When the youngsters are ready to leave the nest the cardinal family may put on quite a show. A friend of mine called one day to invite me to the "coming-out party" of a group of three young cardinals that were ready to fledge from a nest in a hanging basket on her patio.

When I arrived on the scene one fledgling was perched on the rim of the nest, another was on the wooden fence a few feet away from the basket, and the third was on the ground eight or ten feet away from the parents. The parents were vociferous in their efforts at encouraging the three. Loud "*chinks*" were coming from both parties. One or the other of the parents took a few steps toward the fledgling on the ground, uttered several insistent "*chinks*," then turned and hopped away from it. If the baby refused to move, the adult repeated the procedure until the youngster made an effort to come toward the parent. After several moments of urging, the fledgling spread its tiny wings and feebly flew to a tree, where it alighted several feet from the ground.

After that accomplishment the parents concentrated on the "fence" bird. "*Chink! Chink! Chink!*" the parents called repeatedly. The fledgling finally made the long flight from the top of the fence to the ground. Each time one of the young made an advance, the parents appeared to praise it with lavish "*chinks*." Finally, all three of the young were out of the nest. The parents then led the fledglings into a thicket and out of our sight.

During the early days of fledglinghood, the parents go to great efforts to keep the young out of harm's way. Hiding them in a thicket until they are capable fliers is one method they use to protect the brood. I never see young that are right out of the nest at my feeders. It is usually after the young have reached almost adult size that family groups begin to forage together.

The fledgling stage is defined as the period between the time the bird leaves the nest and the time when it becomes completely independent of parental care. Here again, the period is characterized by dramatic changes and rapid growth. It would be interesting if one could follow the family just described for the next three weeks, the normal length of time young are dependent upon the adults. During this period, the male parent continues to oversee care of the brood if they are the first of the season, teaching them survival skills that will help protect them for the rest of their lives. While this is happening, the female builds another nest and starts another brood. If it is the final brood of the season, both parents share equally in the care of the young until they are independent.

Texas naturalist Roy Bedichek told an interesting story about a mother cardinal teaching her young their table manners. He said he was often accused of "nature-faking" on account of the story, but he maintained that this actually happened. During watermelon season, he observed that the cardinals he fed loved watermelon seeds, so he made a practice of saving and curing them for his redbirds. Since watermelon seeds are similar to sunflower seeds, the mother cracked each seed, extracted the kernel, and nipped off a small bit for each of her young. While the mother was cracking the seeds, the babies gathered around her and waited impatiently for their turn to be fed. One morning it seemed that one of the youngsters was more impatient than the others and kept rushing forward to get the morsel from his mother's bill. Finally, the mother got tired of his aggression and gave him a sharp peck on the head and drove him out of the circle. It seemed the mother was trying to teach the baby a lesson in patience as well as manners.

Bedichek said he finally quit telling the story because it sounded so preposterous, until a friend of his told him a similar story that involved a cardinal and a House Sparrow. A male cardinal was preparing to feed his young from a piece of hard toast when he turned his back on the baby. While his back was turned, a House Sparrow flew down and stole the toast from the cardinal. The adult cardinal, thinking it was his youngster who had stolen the bread, promptly trounced the baby, not realizing the sparrow was the real culprit.

During the breeding season of 1991, Dr. Fred Gehlbach observed some behavior that he had never seen before in his twenty years of research on cardinals. Here is how the series of events developed. A pair of cardinals built their first nest of the season three feet from the ground in a small red cedar tree. Four young successfully fledged from this nest. Two weeks later, a second nest was started in a deciduous holly, about thirty feet away from the first nest. Four young successfully fledged from this nest about the middle of June. It was this brood that was so interesting to watch.

When the young from the second brood were about one week old, the female parent started construction on a third nest in a plum tree directly in front of Gehlbach's house. (All three nests were within a thirty- to forty-foot radius of the house.) The parents fed the second brood throughout the third incubation period. For about a week after the third brood hatched,

To help sanitize the nest, this parent removes a fecal sac directly from the nestling's vent.

the second set of chicks continued to beg food from the parents on the ground through the shrubbery that surrounded the third nest tree, but the parents ignored them. Gehlbach said that was when the strange behavior began.

Chicks from the second brood started going directly to the nest when they saw the parents feeding their younger siblings. They sat and begged, and the male parent distributed the food he brought to the nest equally between the nestlings and the fledglings. In the midst of all this commotion, one chick from the third brood hopped out of the nest prematurely at the age of eight days and refused to go back. For the next few days this would-be fledgling flapped its wings a lot but never tried to fly. It just hopped around on the limbs near the nest, and both parents fed it every time they fed the three that remained in the nest. By the time this brood fledged, the male parent had finally succeeded in driving away the young of the second brood.

I have witnessed, through the years, countless cardinal families outside my windows—young at different stages of development accompanied by parents. I have seen them develop from wing-fluttering, begging young to independent individuals thirty-eight to forty-five days old and able to forage on their own. I have watched as the youngsters were transformed from helpless creatures with drab brown plumage and dark bills to juvenile birds mottled brown and red. As they matured further, their bills became coral red, and their feathers turned to golden brown or brilliant red, according to their sex. Having cardinals nest near your home provides the rare privilege of observing close at hand such scenes in the bird's life history.

Brood Parasitism

As already pointed out, the cardinal has a number of enemies. Snakes prey on cardinal eggs, and furred enemies include raccoons, fox squirrels, and cats among others that seem to make a habit of eating cardinal eggs and/or young. Among their feathered enemies is a surprising array of species: Sharp-shinned and Cooper's hawks prey on weak individuals; Blue Jays raid cardinal nests and do away with eggs and young; House Wrens sometimes puncture cardinal eggs; Eastern Screech-Owls eat unsuspecting individuals as they feed at dawn and dusk; and Gray Catbirds and House Sparrows are among the most competitive for nesting sites.

Perhaps one of the most unusual enemies of the cardinal is the cowbird, a bird that parasitizes other birds' nests. The female cowbird lays her eggs in the nests of other species and leaves all parental duties to the host species. The cardinal, especially in the central portions of its range, is a fairly common victim of the Brown-headed Cowbird.

Picture this scenario that I often see outside my own windows during nesting season: A young bird flutters its wings in food-begging fashion as it stands before an adult cardinal. The cardinal cracks open a sunflower seed, extracts the nutmeat, and places it in the mouth of the young bird that is obviously not a cardinal.

How do I know it is not a cardinal? In the first place, it has no hint of a crest. Second, its bill is definitely not shaped like a cardinal's. It is a Brown-headed Cowbird fledgling instead. Then why, you may ask, is the cardinal feeding one that is not of its own kind? The answer is, the cardinal parents were victims of *brood parasitism.*

It would be easy to hate the cowbird. It always irritates me when I look out my window and see a cardinal feeding a young Brown-headed Cowbird, because I know exactly what has happened. While the female cardinal was away from her nest, the female cowbird stole in, removed a cardinal egg, laid her similar white egg speckled with brown, and left it for the unsuspecting foster parent to incubate and raise the young as her own.

The cowbird nestling has the advantage of size from the very beginning because cowbird eggs require only eleven to twelve days of incubation and the cardinal's require twelve or more. Add to its advantage of size its aggression. When the foster parents bring food to the nest, it usually outreaches its nest mates and is the first to be fed. As a result, the cowbird grows more rapidly than the cardinal nestlings. Sometimes it crowds out the smaller young cardinals, often trampling them to death

The female cowbird lays her slightly larger egg (upper right egg) in the nest of the cardinal (as well as numerous other species) and leaves all parental responsibilities to the host parent.

or knocking them out of the nest. When this happens, instead of flying to the ground with food for its own young, the parent ignores the outcast nestling and fills the gaping mouth of the foster child that now dominates the nest.

Irritation is the common reaction among those who observe brood parasitism. It seems natural to abhor the parasite and pity the victim. The truth of the matter is that this practice is a highly developed means of survival for the parasitic species and causes no appreciable cost to *most* of the host species. *Most* but not *all*. The cowbird has caused considerable damage to the populations of such endangered species as the Black-capped Vireo, Golden-cheeked Warbler, and Kirtland's Warbler. But that is another story entirely.

The foster parent does have options. It may merely accept the strange object found in its nest whether it is similar to its own eggs or not. (This is usually the case with cardinals.) It can eject the egg, as American Robins do. It may cover the egg or eggs by adding new nesting materials, thus adding new layers to its nest. There is at least one case on record of a cardinal building a two-story nest. The lower floor contained two cowbird eggs. Rarely, the host may attack the unwanted nestling, or it may abandon the nest and build a new one in a different location. But, generally speaking, the urge to brood and feed overcomes all other drives, and the host incubates the egg and rears the cowbird at the expense of the life of at least one of its own young. And so it goes with cardinals in my own backyard.

Oklahoma ornithologist George M. Sutton declared the Northern Cardinal to be the cowbird's perfect "host" in that state. But, according to his observations there from the late 1950s through the late 1970s, he concluded that brood parasitism does not eliminate the cardinal because the cardinal usually succeeds in rearing at least one of its own young for every one, two, or three cowbirds it rears. So even though I may be infuriated when I see a Northern Cardinal feeding a baby cowbird, the status of *Cardinalis cardinalis* remains intact.

That birds spend a good deal of time preening, dusting, oiling, and otherwise caring for their feathers is no surprise: feathers are probably the most important pieces of avian apparatus.
—Jack Page and Eugene S. Morton, *Lords of the Air*

August and September: Molting and Maintaining Feathers

*B*irds are unique in the animal world in that they develop feathers. No other animal has feathers, and no bird in the world lacks the ability to develop feathers. One of the earliest birds of which we have fossil evidence is the Archaeopteryx. It lived 160 million years ago. The imprints of its feathers in the fine limestone in which it was found show that they were exactly like the feathers of birds of modern times. The feather is an ancient structure indeed.

Feathers serve many purposes. They act as insulators against cold. They protect the bird's skin from sun, rain, and injury. In most species they enable the bird to fly. In some cases they provide protective coloration so that the bird is camouflaged in its environment. In many species, as in cardinals, the color of feathers denotes the bird's sex. Colorful patches of feathers on some birds play an important role in courtship displays and in territorial battles. Birds produce feathers not only in an array of colors, but also in large numbers. The average ranges from close to one thousand feathers on hummingbirds to more than twenty-five thousand on swans. In short, feathers are very important to birds and contribute up to 12 percent of a bird's weight.

Even though feathers are light and look fragile, they are actually quite durable. Ounce for ounce, feathers are among the most durable structures on Earth. One of birds' most time-consuming activities is maintenance behavior—keeping their feathers in prime condition. They have several ways of doing this: bathing (in pools of water, in dew or condensed fog, in rain, in dust, and in sunlight), preening, oiling, and anting. Cardinals engage in all these activities.

First let us consider water bathing. Since bathing functions as a means of keeping the plumage in order and rarely is done just for cleaning purposes, birds need to bathe in winter as well as in summer. If you have a birdbath in your garden, keep fresh

Like children, cardinals seem to enjoy bathing in the spray of lawn sprinklers.

water in it year-round and you will probably see this act often. First the cardinal (or other bird) steps into the container, wades in with both feet to a depth of about one inch, ruffles the feathers all over its body, lowers its head into the water, and raises it abruptly, flipping droplets of water over its back and wings. It may even dip its wings in the water and swish them around. Then it shakes itself all over, much as a dog does to dry itself and rearrange its fur. Sometimes the bird repeats these actions several times before it flies up and out of the water. Since a wet bird cannot fly quickly to safety, it is important to place your birdbath near cover—under a bush or close to a tree with overhanging limbs, for example—so the bird can escape from cats and other predators.

When birdbaths are not available, birds find other places to bathe. Small birds bathe in the shallow edges of ponds and streams, in snowmelt, or in puddles after a rain. During times of drought, birds have been observed bathing in dew or condensed fog that collects on leaves or on grass. During a drought in Tennessee in 1966, observers watched four female and two male cardinals as they bathed on dew-covered leaves in the crowns of sassafras, red maple, and willow trees. Dousing themselves with the refreshing droplets, the birds went through all the motions of a full bath.

Researcher Amelia R. Laskey once observed a cardinal standing on her driveway while a steady rain was falling. She said the bird shook its wings and tail as though bathing in a pool or birdbath. Like children, many birds seem to enjoy bathing in the spray of lawn sprinklers—from robins, cardinals, towhees, and thrashers to hummingbirds. My friend Pam Moes periodically turns on her lawn sprinkler specifically for this purpose during the summer. Barbara Garland happened to be visiting Pam one day and was able to photograph a female cardinal bathing in the spray while it perched on the branch of a tree.

Kenneth Lowe of Yukon, Oklahoma, relates a story of how he discovered that cardinals enjoy this type of shower. He was watering the summer-parched corn in his garden one day, when he noticed a female cardinal clinging to one of the stalks. When he turned off the water, she flew to the ground for a drink. When she didn't fly away, he decided to try something. At the risk of frightening the bird, he adjusted the hose nozzle to spray and pointed it directly at the bird. He said instead of frightening her, this seemed to be exactly what she had wanted all along, and she proceeded to wash herself in the soft spray. Soon the male cardinal flew down for a drink and then turned his attention to Lowe. While the bird stared at him from a distance of fifteen feet, Lowe turned the hose in his direction and gave the crimson male a thorough dousing. The bird returned to the spray four times before flying to a treetop to preen.

Some species of birds bathe in dust. First they make a shallow scrape, peck in the dirt to loosen it, and then roll their bodies in the dirt and toss dust particles over their wings and backs like droplets of water. I have observed House Sparrows dust bathing in a neighbor's flower bed, but I have never seen cardinals do this. Alexander Wetmore reports one instance when sparrows were unable to find dust to bathe in, and settled for a bowl of sugar.

Late in the nineteenth century, Henry Nehrling observed, "During summer, especially in the late afternoon, the cardinals are often seen dusting themselves in the country roads, near Osage orange and Cherokee rose hedges." Although I have no documented proof, I can only imagine that the nature of some parts of their range in the desert Southwest forces cardinals to resort to this type of bathing. Investigators don't know why birds use this dry shampoo method. Some think it improves the alignment of the barbs on the feathers and helps to dislodge parasites. Whatever the reason, it is fascinating to watch.

Have you ever seen a cardinal or other bird emerge from a shady area into full sunlight and suddenly drop to the ground as if injured or ill? I observed one such cardinal as it crouched low with its belly touching the ground, ruffled its crown feathers, opened its tail feathers like a fan, flopped its spread wings to the ground, and tilted its body to one side, all the while panting with its mouth open. With its back to the sun it remained in this awkward position for several minutes. Cardinals have been observed in this position for a full fifteen minutes in one patch of sunshine. Upon seeing such a sight, you may wonder if the bird is dying of heat stroke, but in fact it is simply sunbathing. Many avian species are known to sunbathe in hot weather and in cold.

Like human sun worshipers all over the world, birds, too, enjoy "soaking up some rays." However, unlike humans, whose skin may be harmed by the ultraviolet rays, birds benefit greatly from their moments in the sun. The bird's body and skin absorb the ultraviolet radiation and stimulate vitamin D production. Some think heat and light may cause parasites that have been hiding deep within the feathers to move to places where the bird can more easily remove them by scratching or preening. Sunshine helps dry feathers after a rain shower or a bath, and during molting when the skin is irritated, it provides a source of energy and comfort.

Feathers have a shaft, or quill, that runs through the middle. On each side of the shaft are vanes with thousands of minute interlocking barbs. When these barbs become ruffled or separated, birds must use their bills to zip them back together. This behavior is called *preening,* and it is the most important single act a bird performs in the care and maintenance of its feathers. It is something that must be done every day of a bird's life.

Preening usually follows bathing. You probably have observed it often among the cardinals, jays, and other birds that frequent your yard. First, the cardinal fluffs up all the feathers in the section it is preening. Then it takes each individual feather in its bill and, beginning at the base and moving to the tip, gently bites and strokes it until all the barbs are smoothed and locked back together again. It probes meticulously under the outer feathers to remove dust and parasites. At times a bird must become a contortionist to preen the hard-to-reach parts of its body. For the head and neck feathers that need attention a bird uses its feet to smooth down the feathers.

Barbara Garland said that the one-footed cardinals she observed in her yard had difficulty preening. With one foot missing, they found it hard to balance. She said each bird used its stub to scratch its head.

Most birds have an oil gland called the *uropygial,* or preen, gland. It is located just above the base of the tail. If you have ever plucked and cleaned a domestic chicken, you know what I am describing. It is a yellowish white lump with a nipplelike orifice. This gland secretes a solution that birds use in preening their feathers. In order to reach it, the bird twists its neck until it can touch the gland with its bill. As if dipping a pen in an inkwell, the bird touches the gland with the tip of its bill and transfers the oil to its feathers with rubbing movements. To oil the feathers that cannot be reached with its bill—the head, for example—the bird transfers oil from its bill to its feet and then rubs its head with its feet. The oil helps waterproof the plumage and helps maintain the feathers' insulating properties by keeping them from drying out and becoming brittle. It also helps to keep the bill in good condition. Some authorities believe the oil acts as an antibacterial and fungicidal agent as well.

Cardinals and many other birds have a curious habit called *anting*—placing crushed or live ants among their feathers, rubbing them through their feathers, or allowing them to crawl through their feathers. When the ants are finished, the birds' plumage looks wet. Many authorities believe that birds use the formic acid secreted by ants to help rid their bodies of lice, mites, and other parasites that give them discomfort and to relieve skin irritation during molting. Other researchers suggest that ant secretions may increase the flow of saliva for use in preening, help in removing stale preen oil, or increase feather wear resistance. More than two hundred kinds of birds worldwide practice anting.

Occasionally birds use substitutes in their "anting" behavior. Some observers have noted the following materials that birds use in the same manner as ants: beetles, mealworms, the flesh of lemons, orange juice, coffee, vinegar, beer, cigarette and cigar butts, hot chocolate, soapsuds, mothballs, and sumac berries.

Feathers are simply horny outgrowths of the skin much the same as our fingernails. Blood carries food and oxygen to the feather through the opening at the base of the shaft. Once a feather has reached its full growth, this opening closes, shutting off its supply of life-giving elements. Then the feather becomes a dead structure. It cannot be repaired if it becomes damaged or broken through wear. However, if for any reason a bird loses an entire feather between molts, a new feather begins to form immediately.

As a young bird matures it goes through several different plumage changes before attaining its adult plumage. In the first few days of its life it loses its natal down and puts on juvenal plumage with which it leaves the nest as a fledgling. In the following weeks it sheds those feathers in exchange for a more mature appearance. Thereafter, most adult birds molt, or shed old feathers and replace them with new, at least once a year. Some molt twice or three times yearly. A few species are known to molt four times a year.

Typically, all feathers on a bird's body are replaced after the breeding season. This is when cardinals seem to disappear from our gardens and stop singing. It almost seems as if they do not want us to see or hear them while they molt. I must admit I could sympathize: they do look rather weird while replacing their finery.

In August one year a puzzled friend called to tell me there was a "black-headed cardinal" feeding in his backyard. When I asked him if he was sure it was a cardinal, he said the bird definitely had a cardinal-like beak, and the rest of its body plumage was typically "cardinal." The thing that puzzled him most was that it had no crest. This crestless cardinal was, in fact, a cardinal that was molting. It had lost the feathers on its head, and the dark skin underneath gave it the appearance of indeed being "black-headed."

But this is not the norm. Fortunately, normal molting is a gradual process rather than an instantaneous one, and most birds maintain adequate plumage protection and the power of flight. Usually birds don't lose all the feathers of one area of the body at the same time. If you could examine the skin of a plucked bird you would note the pits, or follicles, from which the feathers grow. They are not distributed evenly over the bird's body, but rather they are grouped into definite areas called feather tracts. The feathers of a particular tract are normally not lost all at once. In songbirds the process takes place in a wave, beginning with the head, face, and throat, and extending backward gradually, with right and left sides at the same stage simultaneously.

Typically, in most flying birds, the flight feathers are shed and replaced one by one in orderly fashion so that flight is still possible even though a few feathers are missing. Usually, the innermost primary feather on each wing is the first to go. As soon as its replacement begins to grow, the one next to it drops out, and so on, until all flight feathers have been replaced. And it is the same way with the rest of the bird's body, tract by tract.

In a few groups of flying birds all flight feathers are lost simultaneously, so that, temporarily, they are incapable of flight. Loons, grebes, swans, geese, and ducks follow this pattern. When this happens they are naturally vulnerable and literally must go into hiding to protect themselves from harm until flight capability is restored.

With adult cardinals molting usually begins after their last brood has hatched, which is about the middle of August where I live in Central Texas. By late September, molting is complete in most birds around my home. In a notebook that I keep near my favorite bird window, I find these entries:

"August 15: Both adult cardinals look really ragged, with dark patches scattered all over their bodies where feathers are missing."

"August 30: Adult male cardinal looks as if his molt is almost complete. Adult female still a little ragged around head and neck; and flight feathers are not fully grown—wings still very short."

"September 10: Adult cardinals look as if molt is complete— both really handsome in their new finery. Mother still feeding one black-billed young. All three at feeder after rain shower."

"September 11: Saw a young male cardinal almost in full adult plumage. Bill almost totally red. Also saw one young that still has an all-black bill." (Bill color change requires about a month.)

Remember, a songbird the size of a cardinal has thousands of feathers that it must preen every day. This causes a terrific drain of energy, and *replacing* that many feathers at least once a year requires great energy output as well. Since feathers are made up entirely of protein and comprise 4 to 12 percent of the bird's weight, any food supplement we supply during their time of molting is put to good use by the birds in our gardens—another reason for providing food and water for cardinals and other birds of our neighborhoods through every season of the year.

Cardinals usually gather together in flocks in fall and winter, staying in areas where food is plentiful.
    —Donald and Lillian Stokes, *A Guide to Bird Behavior*

October through December: When Birds of a Feather Flock Together

*O*ne evening in late November, I looked out my favorite bird window and saw a spectacle not soon to be forgotten—ten pairs of cardinals foraging beneath the sunflower feeder in my backyard. It looked as if someone had scattered on my lawn twenty colorful blossoms. Although I shall long remember that scene, it is not unusual at this time of year to see anywhere from four to sixty or more cardinals in a group. This is called *flocking behavior,* and it is common after the end of breeding season when the last of the juveniles become independent. These flocks, containing both juveniles and adults, remain together throughout early winter and don't break up until February and March.

"Birds of a feather flock together," and why not when flocking has advantages? Number one: because a flock has more eyes and ears than one individual bird, protection against predators is more efficient. A bird in a flock is less likely to be surprised by a hawk or an owl than when it is alone. Just go to a woodland edge in fall or winter, imitate the call of an Eastern Screech-Owl, and see what happens. Immediately, a mixed flock of curious birds—usually including several cardinals—comes out of hiding to mob the unwelcome intruder. The enemy, if it were a real owl, might be intimidated by such numbers and move to a different perch, but it seldom leaves its territory when mobbed. Thus we see mobbing used by flocks of small birds to warn predators rather than to repel them.

Number two: a bird in a flock is less likely to overlook sources of food than when it is alone, whether they are sunflower seeds in a backyard, for example, or natural foods that are abundant during winter months. I cannot stress too much the importance of dependable food sources for birds during cold weather. Fat is not only fuel for birds; it also gives them added layers of insulation against the cold. Cardinals are no exception. They, like most resident North American birds, store layers of fat in sequence and thus build up deposits in different parts of their bodies over time. First, they lay down fat in the neck pouch that is located between the breast muscles. Next, fat overlays the abdomen, then forms under the wings, and ultimately encircles many of the internal organs. Thus the cardinal buys time that helps it to survive under severe weather conditions. It can normally carry about three days' worth of reserve fat—enough to get it through an average ice storm or blizzard. If the cardinal cannot find food by the fourth day, it begins to starve, and death follows swiftly.

Number three: the more birds that roost (sleep) together during severely cold weather, the warmer the individuals will be. In much the same manner as people, birds huddle close together to draw warmth from the bodies of other birds and thus are able to survive long, cold winter nights. Just at dusk you may see cardinals flying singly or in small groups to these roosts, which are often in dense evergreen thickets.

In 1832 Thomas Nuttall, the noted botanical explorer and ornithologist, observed a flock in South Carolina: "in severe weather, at sunset, . . . I observed a flock [of cardinals] passing to a roost . . . which continued, in lengthened file, to fly over my head at a considerable height for more than twenty minutes together . . . and, at daybreak, they were seen again to proceed and disperse for subsistence." He was struck by the beauty of the procession as the last rays of the setting sun "flashed upon their brilliant livery."

The number of birds in these winter flocks remains rather constant. Although individuals may separate themselves from the group, generally they are soon replaced by others. Usually the flocks are fairly evenly divided by sex, but the male cardinals may be slightly dominant over the females, especially in feeding situations. Domestic chickens observe a social hierarchy, or "pecking order," among themselves. Dominant chickens peck subordinates in a certain order without fear of retaliation. It is much the same in a flock of cardinals. Bird A pecks B, C, and D; B pecks C and D; C pecks D; and D pecks no one. A is dominant; D is most subordinate.

At first this pecking order may seem to constitute cruel treatment of the subordinates; but actually, it is advantageous for the individuals as well as for the group as a whole. It lends stability to the group and eliminates fighting for food and water. All members know their places, and each is able to obtain the necessities of life.

In any flock of cardinals, or other birds for that matter, birds maintain an almost equal distance between each other. This phenomenon is known as *individual distance*. No matter how large or small the flock or the size of the area they occupy, each bird always seems to manage to preserve a certain amount of space around itself into which no other bird dares to move.

Even though this may be the season of flocking, don't be surprised if you see a single pair of cardinals at your feeder throughout the winter months. Some cardinals choose not to join a flock, but rather to remain on their breeding grounds, as a pair, through the winter. If you are lucky enough to see a flock of these splendid birds, remember that this is normal behavior for this time of year. I cannot think of a winter scene that is more striking than a flock of cardinals perched in a bare winter tree or shrub or a flock silhouetted against the backdrop of an evergreen. At such a time they look like ornaments on a Christmas tree, and we can be glad that "birds of a feather" do, indeed, "flock together."

Life Expectancy

Often when birds forage and nest in our yards, we claim "ownership" of them and consequently feel a certain degree of responsibility for their well-being. We offer them shelter, water, and nourishing food; we may even try to protect them from such predators as neighborhood cats or bird-eating hawks. We wish for them long, healthy lives.

Just how long can cardinals be expected to live? Generally speaking, the smaller the bird, the shorter its life expectancy; the larger the bird, the longer its life expectancy. If a young bird can survive the first year of life, it may be expected to live a surprisingly long time. Barring accidental death, birds live longer than mammals of similar size. During its first year a bird faces incredible hazards and adversities. Nest predation even before hatching, predation while still in the nest, brood parasitism, extreme weather conditions, accidents, diseases, starvation, encounters with enemies both furred and feathered—all are perils faced by birds in the wild. It is surprising that any survive to maturity.

Precise information on the longevity of birds is not easy to procure. Most of the information we have is gathered from bird-banding data. *Banding* is the term used in America for placing aluminum bands on the legs of wild birds in order to trace their times of migration, behavior, flying routes, destinations, local movements, population changes, and length of life. In Great Britain and Europe the practice is called *ringing.*

Life expectancy, the number of years that a species may be expected to live in the wild, varies dramatically from *longevity,* the natural or potential life span of a bird if it is not killed by an accident or disease. Life expectancy is much shorter than longevity because of the incredible number of hazards in a wild bird's life. In Gehlbach's study of cardinals in Central Texas, of the banded adults, an alarming 94 percent were not seen again in a year or less after banding; but their exact ages at banding were not known in most cases. Among the survivors known to live 2 years or more, fifteen males lived an average of 4.3 years (maximum, 10.1 years). Fourteen females lived 3.5 years (maximum, 10.2 years).

In a study by Amelia R. Laskey of 1,135 cardinals whose life span could have been 3 or more years, only thirty (2.6 percent) reached the age of 3 to 6 years. Her oldest female was 4.5 years of age, and two males reached 6 years. She cites from the literature a female that was 10 years of age and a male 13.5 years old. Her report indicates that this older bird was banded in February 1924 and was last seen in November 1936, when he appeared to be very feeble, although he had mated and reared a brood that year. In one study the maximum recorded life span of the Northern Cardinal in the wild is 15 years and 9 months.

Birds in captivity seem to live longer than those who live in natural surroundings. Of course, they are protected from most of the hazards faced by birds in the wild. A captive cardinal, raised as a house pet in Atlanta, Georgia, lived to the ripe old age of 28.5 years. So you see, if we could find a way to protect our favorite redbird in the wild, it has the potential for a very long life.

Through yet another window you will see how the popularity of this flamboyant red bird affects American culture: as state symbol, athletic mascot, and object of art and literature.

PART 2

The Cardinal in American Culture

Purple lilacs nodding in a New England dooryard, the rich scent
of yellow jessamine adrift on the southern night, a loon's laughter
echoing eerily across a still lake, stout cactus lifting a crown of
pale blossoms to the desert sun, rhododendrons aflame in the
misty coolness of northwestern slopes, the meadowlark's sweet,
wild song flung on the prairie wind, a cardinal's vivid scarlet
flashing against forest green . . .

—The 1982 Fifty State Birds and Flowers Mint Set

The Cardinal as Icon

Well-known poets such as Robert Penn Warren, Walt Whitman, Emily Dickinson, and James Whitcomb Riley, as well as uncounted local versifiers affirm the affection Americans hold for their natural surroundings. The writings of Ralph Waldo Emerson, Henry David Thoreau, John Burroughs, Annie Dillard, and Rachel Carson, to name a few—all urge us to see ourselves as a part of nature, not apart from it. Even Tin Pan Alley melodies, folk songs, barbershop ballads, and show tunes reflect America's love for the birds and flowers that embellish our lives with living beauty.

In 1893 the idea of state flowers was born at the World's Columbian Exposition in Chicago when various women's groups decorated each state's exhibits with flowers native to that state. At the fair a women's organization proposed that a national garland of flowers be selected. Each flower was to be chosen by the people of that state and adopted by the state's legislature. Seven years later bird lovers suggested adopting state birds as well.

Soon campaigns were launched nationwide until each state had selected at least one favorite bird as its avian symbol. Some chose two. In all, thirty two different species have been named as state birds. In some cases a bird was chosen for economic or patriotic reasons, but typically a bird was selected by sheer popularity based on aesthetic reasons. From 1926 through the early 1930s Audubon societies and women's clubs all over the nation fueled the public's interest in this project by holding popular votes, many of them among schoolchildren.

The Northern Cardinal proved to be the favorite bird, being chosen by seven states. Kentucky led the way when the "Kentucky Cardinal" was declared the official state bird by the legislature in 1926. Six other states followed Kentucky's lead in choosing the cardinal. Illinois was second, in 1929, after a poll of the state's schoolchildren in which the cardinal received 39,226 votes. The Eastern Bluebird was the closest contender with 30,306 votes.

Four years later, in 1933, Ohio joined the ranks of cardinal devotees. A decade later North Carolina voted in the cardinal. West Virginia did so in 1949, Virginia followed suit a year later in 1950, and Indiana in 1963 became the seventh state to adopt this crimson beauty as its state bird.

The U.S. Postal Service got into the act when it issued an attractive set of stamps honoring the state birds and flowers of all fifty states in 1982. The stamps were designed by the first father-son team ever to design a U.S. issue, Arthur and Alan Singer of Jericho, New York. The father, Arthur, created the bird designs, and Alan, the flowers.

Out of curiosity I checked the statistics of the ninetieth Christmas Bird Count (the latest available at the time of this writing) to determine the number of cardinals counted in the seven states that have chosen the Northern Cardinal as their official state bird. Keep in mind that each "count area" is a circle with a 15-mile diameter, or roughly 177 square miles. By no means do these numbers reflect the total number of cardinals that reside in each state mentioned.

My unscientific study revealed the following: Out of 54,550 cardinals counted in these seven states, West Virginia was at the bottom of the heap with 2,480 cardinals at thirteen different sites. Kentucky came in sixth, with 2,940 at eleven sites. Next was North Carolina with 4,521 cardinals counted in thirty-two locations. Indiana won the fourth spot when counters tallied 7,997 cardinals. Illinois placed third with 9,737 cardinals at forty-one sites. Virginia came in second with 10,395 of its favorite redbirds found in thirty-eight different count areas. The landslide victory was won by Ohio, where 16,480 cardinals were counted at fifty-four sites.

Love for the cardinal, the most common garden bird of eastern North America, is reflected in more ways than state symbols and U.S. postage stamps. It has also invaded the athletic arenas of our nation. Baseball's St. Louis Cardinals in the National League and the Phoenix Cardinals in the National Football League are two professional athletic teams that have adopted the cardinal as mascot or symbol. Baseball teams in other leagues found the cardinal attractive as well—the Savannah Cardinals of Georgia, the Front Royal Cardinals of Virginia, the Orleans Cardinals of Massachusetts, the Hutchinson Cardinals of Kansas, the Johnson City Cardinals of Tennessee, and the Peoria Cardinals of Peoria, Arizona. Florida and Kentucky each boast teams affiliated with the St. Louis Cardinals—the St. Petersburg Cardinals and the Louisville Redbirds.

The roster of teams choosing other bird names reads like a checklist of North American birds. A survey of two thousand junior and senior colleges of the United States and Canada discloses that seventy-two schools chose the eagle to represent them on the playing field. Various other birds that proved to be among the most popular were blue jays, seahawks, roadrunners, owls, and—you guessed it—cardinals. Of the schools surveyed, twenty-two—seven junior colleges and fifteen senior colleges—have adopted the cardinal as the symbol or mascot for their school's athletic teams.

The stories of how these colleges decided to adopt the bird reveals some interesting anecdotes. In 1884 Wesleyan University in Middletown, Connecticut, voted to discard lavender as the college color in favor of the more striking cardinal red and black. However, shortly after World War I, the red uniforms became maroon because of a careless error by the manufacturers, and maroon remained their color for several years. In 1925 an Alumni Council referendum reestablished cardinal red as "the shade that makes the strongest, most inspiring contrast with black."

About the same time, many students were seeking a name other than "the Methodists" as the designation for Wesleyan athletes. In 1925 the student body named their literature magazine *The Wesleyan Cardinal,* and a color reproduction of the bird was printed on the cover. Finally, Walter Fricke of the class of 1933 bought a baseball jacket with a cardinal on the breast pocket. The students liked the emblem, and since they were tired of newspaper reporters referring to their gridders as "the mysterious ministers from Middletown," they soon decided to designate their athletes the Cardinals.

As early as 1897 a campus-wide publication at State University College in New York was called *The Cardinal.* A comical portrayal of the Plattsburgh Cardinal, symbol of the school, usually is shown wearing sneakers, but when used in connection with the hockey team the cartoonish cardinal switches his footwear to ice skates.

The University of Louisville's athletic symbol and school colors of cardinal and black were chosen sometime after 1913 to honor Kentucky's official state bird. Their athletic teams became known as the Fighting Cardinals sometime after 1921.

Illinois State's athletic squads have been known as the Redbirds since 1923 when then-athletic director Clifford E. "Pop" Horton and *Daily Pantagraph* sports editor Fred Young collaborated to change the nickname from Teachers. When Horton first went to ISU he began calling the teams Cardinals because of the school colors—cardinal red and white. Young, who was ISU's 1910 basketball captain, later changed the name to Redbirds in his newspaper headlines to avoid confusion with the St. Louis Cardinals baseball team.

Catholic University of America, in Washington, D.C., originally named its teams the Red and Black for the school colors. In 1925 a contest supported by the school newspaper determined that the name should be changed to the Cardinals.

At Ball State University in Muncie, Indiana, there was growing discontent in 1927, over the use of the nickname Hoosieroons. This prompted the school newspaper to sponsor a contest to select a new name with a five-dollar gold piece for the prize. Still, no suitable name was chosen, and one week later, coaches Paul "Billy" Williams and Norman Wann were discussing possibilities. Williams, a loyal fan of the St. Louis Cardinals, commented that he liked the cardinal insignia on a sweatshirt worn by National Baseball Hall of Fame's Rogers Hornsby. Later Williams formally submitted the name for consideration. Another student election was held later that month, and the Cardinal was proclaimed the winner by a landslide.

Saginaw Valley State at University Center, Michigan, chose the cardinal symbol by default. A contest sponsored by the student government determined that Voyagers should be the name of their athletic teams. However, students, faculty, and administration were not really satisfied with this name and decided to accept the first runner-up in the contest—Cardinals—since the school's color had always been cardinal red. After that several cardinal logos were used on the campus until 1974 when the school fielded its first football team. A cartoonish Big Red was adopted at that time and used until 1978 when a new stylized version replaced it. The new Big Red is a symbol for both the men's and women's sports activities.

Other schools and colleges that use the nickname are Catonville Community College in Baltimore, Maryland; Henderson County Junior College in Athens, Texas; Hibbing College, Hibbing, Minnesota; Labette Community Junior College in Parsons, Kansas; Mineral Area Junior College in Flat River, Missouri; North Central College, Naperville, Illinois; Lamar University, Beaumont, Texas; St. John Fisher College, Rochester, New York; and Iowa State University of Science and Technology, Ames, Iowa.

Surprisingly, some schools that are located in places where the Northern Cardinal does not occur chose the crimson beauty to represent them—North Idaho College in Coeur d'Alene is one, and Skagit Valley College in Mount Vernon, Washington, has teams called Cardinals and Lady Cardinals. In the survey, no explanation is given about the origin of the nickname for either of these schools other than the clue of their school colors.

In 1892 Stanford University's student body chose cardinal red as the official school color, and soon thereafter sportswriters began calling Stanford teams the Cardinals, even though *Cardinalis cardinalis* does not occur in the part of California where the school is located. The nickname prevailed until 1930, when the university officially adopted the Indian as its mascot. But that symbol was dropped in 1972 when Stanford's Native Americans met with President Richard W. Lyman and suggested that the Indian was not an appropriate symbol. The president and the student senate agreed and reinstated the nickname Cardinals in reference to their school color.

High schools across North America utilize some variation of a cardinal logo on their uniforms or helmets. They are too numerous to list here, testimony that the popularity of this beautiful red bird is very well established all across the land.

If ever there was a Bird of Christmas, it would have to be the male Northern Cardinal.

—George Harrison, *Sports Afield*

The Cardinal at Christmas

On Christmas Day in 1900, twenty-seven intrepid birders in twenty-six locations, mainly around major northeastern cities, strolled through their designated territories and counted the birds they saw in a twenty-four hour period. Thus was born what is now called the Christmas Bird Count, which takes place every year within a two-week period around Christmas.

Since 1900 the annual event has grown from its original twenty-six locations to more than fifteen hundred, stretching from northernmost Canada to Bogotá, Colombia, to Saipan and Southern Guam. And the participants have increased from the original twenty-seven to well over forty-two thousand who travel by foot, in cars, in marsh buggies, on snowshoes, on skis, in motorized boats, in canoes, in helicopters, in airplanes, and in jeeps, utilizing almost every imaginable mode of travel.

All the information from this annual event is gathered, edited, and reported in *American Birds,* a magazine published under the auspices of the National Audubon Society. Apart from its attraction as a social, sporting, and competitive event, the annual count sheds much light on the early winter distribution of the different species of our native birds—their locations and their numbers. As previously stated, ornithologist Terry Root's analysis of Christmas Bird Count data reveals the northward expansion of the Northern Cardinal over the years.

Root's analysis further reveals that the densest concentrations of cardinals in winter occur on the Mississippi River, both in the South and farther north, and also along the Colorado and Guadalupe rivers in southern Texas. Less dense cardinal populations are found in winter along the Ohio, Arkansas, Brazos, and Red rivers.

No matter how the cardinal ranks in its nationwide abundance according to the Christmas Bird Count of any chosen year, I agree with George Harrison's assessment: "If ever there was a Bird of Christmas, it would have to be the male Northern Cardinal." Walk into any Christmas specialty shop and you will find ample evidence of the popularity of this scarlet beauty as a Christmas symbol. Images ranging from cartoon cardinals to lovely portraits of the bird decorate a wide assortment of Christmas paraphernalia.

You see male cardinals on greeting cards, stationery, paper plates, paper napkins and tablecloths, doormats, light switch plates, candles, candle holders, coffee mugs, plates, glasses, Christmas tree ornaments and lights, bookmarks, mailboxes, Christmas jewelry, and the list goes on and on. Cardinals have become an integral part of the way that many people celebrate the holiday season.

Thero North, a friend of mine who lives in Mercer Island, Washington, conducts her own version of the Christmas Bird Count. She calls it the Christmas Card Bird Count. She performs an actual yearly count and reports that of the cards she receives, more each year feature birds, and about one-quarter of those with birds have cardinals on them. Every year I, too, am the recipient of numerous greeting cards decorated with birds. I have never counted them, but I always save a few— mostly the ones with cardinals. The following verse by Oliver Hereford was on one of my all-time favorite Christmas cards, which featured a pair of cardinals on the front. It expresses my feelings exactly:

> "I heard a bird sing in the dark of December,
> A magical thing and sweet to remember."

Another of my favorite Christmas cards with cardinals contains a verse adapted from a poem by Lord Byron. This one is framed and hangs on my office wall to cheer and inspire throughout the year.

> "A light broke in upon my soul. It was the carol of a bird.
> It ceased and then it came again, the sweetest song ear ever heard."

Every year beginning about the first of December we hear Christmas carols almost everywhere we go—in shopping centers, on car radios, in doctors' offices, in grocery stores, and in our homes. Carols are a part of the celebration of Christmas. But on December 26 something mysterious happens: the sounds of Christmas cease, and suddenly there is a quietus that lasts until the next December. It is almost like the fall quietus that occurs in the bird world at the end of breeding season when most birds cease to sing.

For example, in my own neighborhood, after the cardinals finish their breeding cycle and begin their fall molt, suddenly there are no more cardinal songs to cheer my days. And then one day, "in the dark of December," when I think the silence will never end, the Bird of Christmas, a male Northern Cardinal, bursts forth in song in the backyard, and my world is no longer deprived of his lovely carols. When I hear the long-awaited "*What cheer-cheer-cheer,*" there is a feeling of continuity, as the brilliant red bird once again constructs his invisible song barrier in anticipation of spring and the promise of new life to come. And the seasons in the life of the cardinal begin all over again.

May the sights and sounds of cardinals, from January through December, be "a light . . . upon your soul" in every season of the year, bringing you assurance of continuity and connectedness with the whole of life. May their beauty live in your heart all year—"the sweetest song ear ever heard."

Bibliography

Adams, Marjorie Valentine. In *The Gift of Birds*, ed. H. F. Robinson, Washington, D.C.: 141–142. National Wildlife Federation, 1979.

Bedichek, Roy. *Adventures with a Texas Naturalist*, 183–184. Austin: University of Texas Press, 1961.

Belting, Natalia M. *The Long-tailed Bear (and Other Indian Legends)*, 62–66. New York: Bobbs-Merrill, 1961.

Bent, Arthur Cleveland, and collaborators. *Life Histories of North American Cardinals, Grosbeaks, Buntings, Towhees, Finches, Sparrows, and Allies*, 1–23. U.S. National Museum Bulletin 237. New York: Dover, 1968.

Burroughs, John. *Great Wilderness Days in the Words of John Burroughs*, 63. Waukesha, Wis.: Country Beautiful, 1975.

Choate, Ernest A. *The Dictionary of American Bird Names*. Rev. ed. Harvard, Mass.: Harvard Common Press, 1985.

Conner, Richard N., Mary E. Anderson, and James G. Dickson. "Relationships among Territory Size, Habitat, Song, and Nesting Success of Northern Cardinals." *Auk* 103 (January 1986): 23–31.

Cruickshank, Allen D., and Helen H. *1001 Questions Answered about Birds*. New York: Dover, 1985.

Dennis, John V. *A Complete Guide to Bird Feeding*. New York: Knopf, 1975.

Dixon, Royal. *The Human Side of Birds*. New York: Halcyon House, 1917.

Dow, D. D., and D. M. Scott. "Cardinal Dispersal and Range Expansion." *Canadian Journal of Zoology* 49 (1971): 195–197.

Dunning, John S., with the collaboration of Robert S. Ridgely. *South American Birds: A Photographic Aid to Identification*, 297. Newtown Square, Penn.: Harrowood Books, 1987.

Durant, Mary, and Michael Harwood. *On the Road with John James Audubon*. New York: Dodd, Mead, 1980.

Ehrlich, Paul R., David S. Dobkin, and Darryl Wheye. *The Birder's Handbook: A Field Guide to the Natural History of North American Birds*. New York: Simon & Schuster, 1988.

Franks, Ray. *What's in a Nickname? Exploring the Jungle of College Athletic Mascots*. Amarillo, Tex.: Ray Franks Publishing Ranch, 1982.

"General Notes." *Auk* 91 (April 1974): 418.

"Growth and Age Determination of Nestling Brown-headed Cowbirds." *Wilson Bulletin* 91, no. 3 (September 1979): 464–466.

Harrison, George. "The Cardinal: Big Red." *Sports Afield* (December 1987): 29–30.

James, Ross. *Glen Loates Birds of North America.* Scarborough, Ontario: Prentice-Hall of Canada, 1979.

Johnsgard, Paul A. "Return and Renewal." In *The Wonder of Birds,* 80. Washington, D.C.: National Geographic Society, 1983.

Ladd, Clifton. "Fly-by-Night Parents." *Texas Parks & Wildlife* 49, no. 6 (June 1991): 44–47.

Lemon, Robert E. "The Displays and Call Notes of Cardinals." *Canadian Journal of Zoology* 46 (1968): 141–151.

Lemon, Robert E., and D. M. Scott. "On the Development of Song in Young Cardinals." *Canadian Journal of Zoology* 44 (1966): 192–196.

Lowe, Kenneth. "A Story of Two Special Cardinals." *Bird Watcher's Digest* 1, no. 2 (November/December 1978): 62–64.

Maslowski, Karl. "Share and Share Alike." *WildBird* 5, no. 9 (September 1991): 32–33.

McElroy, Thomas P., Jr. *Habitat Guide to Birding.* New York: Alfred A. Knopf, 1974.

Montroy, A. Sylvia, "Squash, Anyone?" *Bird Watcher's Digest* 3, no. 3 (January/February 1981): 14–17.

Munro, George C. *Hawaii's Birds,* ed. Robert J. Shallenberger. Honolulu: Hawaii Audubon Society, 1978.

Nash, Stephen. "The Songbird Connection." *National Parks* 64, nos. 11–12 (November/December 1990): 23–27.

National Geographic Society. *Field Guide to the Birds of North America.* 2d ed. Washington, D.C.: National Geographic Society, 1987.

Nehrling, Henry. *Our Native Birds of Song and Beauty,* vol. 2, pp. 185–197. Milwaukee: George Brumder, 1896.

"Nest Selection by Brown-headed Cowbirds." *Wilson Bulletin* 91, no. 1 (1979): 118–122.

"Ninetieth Christmas Bird Count." *American Birds* 44, no. 4 (1989).

Nolan, Val, Jr. "Reproductive Success of Birds in Deciduous Scrub Habitat." *Ecology* 44, no. 2 (Spring 1963): 305–313.

Oberholser, Harry C. *The Bird Life of Texas,* edited with distribution maps and additional material by Edgar B. Kincaid, Jr., vol. 2, pp. 853–856. Austin: University of Texas Press, 1974.

Page, Jack, and Eugene S. Morton. *Lords of the Air.* Smithsonian Books, Washington, D.C. Orion Books, New York, 1989.

Pearson, T. Gilbert, editor-in-chief. *Birds of America,* pt. 3, pp. 63–65. Garden City, New York: Garden City Publishing Co., 1917.

Peterson, Roger Tory, and Edward L. Chalif. *A Field Guide to Mexican Birds.* 2d printing with rev. Boston: Houghton Mifflin Company, 1973.

Pettingill, Olin Sewall, Jr. *Ornithology in Laboratory and Field.* Minneapolis, Minn.: Burgess, 1970.

Potter, Eloise F., and Doris C. Hauser. "Relationships of Anting and Sunbathing to Molting in Wild Birds." *Auk* 91 (July 1974): 537–563.

Reilly, Edgar M., and Gorton Carruth. *The Bird Watcher's Diary.* New York: Harper & Row, 1987.

Ritchison, Gary. "The Singing Behavior of Female Northern Cardinals." *The Condor* 88 (1986): 156–159.

———. "Singing of Male Northern Cardinals. *Wilson Bulletin* 100, no. 4 (December 1988): 594–601.

Root, Terry. *Atlas of Wintering North American Birds: An Analysis of Christmas Bird Count Data,* p. 223. Chicago: University of Chicago Press, 1988.

Scheer, George F., ed. *Cherokee Animal Tales,* pp. 62–64. New York: Holiday House, 1968.

Shankle, George Earlie. *State Names, Flags, Seals, Songs, Birds, Flowers, and Other Symbols.* Rev. ed. New York: H. W. Wilson, 1941.

Shearer, Benjamin F., and Barbara S. Shearer. *State Names, Seals, Flags, and Symbols: A Historical Guide.* New York: Greenwood Press, 1987.

Skutch, Alexander. *Parent Birds and Their Young.* Austin: University of Texas Press, 1976.

Stokes, Donald W., and Lillian Q. Stokes. *A Guide to Bird Behavior,* vol. 2, pp. 247–257. Boston: Little, Brown, 1983.

Sutton, George M. *Fifty Common Birds of Oklahoma and the Southern Great Plains,* pp. 86–89. Norman: The University of Oklahoma Press, 1977.

Terres, John K. *The Audubon Society Encyclopedia of North American Birds.* New York: Alfred A. Knopf, 1980.

Torrey, Bradford. "A Bunch of Texas and Arizona Birds." The Texas Collection, vol. 92, no. 549, pp. 96–104. Baylor University Library, Waco, Texas.

Trautman, Milton B. *The Birds of Buckeye Lake, Ohio,* pp. 395–398. Ann Arbor: University of Michigan Press, 1940.

Udvardy, Miklos D. F. *The Audubon Society Field Guide to North American Birds: Western Region,* p. 660. New York: Alfred A. Knopf, 1977.

U.S. Department of the Interior. *The Breeding Bird Survey: Its First Fifteen Years, 1965–1979.* Fish and Wildlife Service, Resource Publication 157. Washington, D.C.: Government Printing Office.

U.S. Postal Service. *The 1982 Fifty State Birds and Flowers Mint Set.* Washington, D.C.: U.S. Government Printing Office, 1983.

Walton, Richard K., and Robert W. Lawson. *Birding by Ear: Eastern/Central.* Boston: Houghton Mifflin, 1989.

Welty, Joel Carl. *The Life of Birds.* New York: Alfred A. Knopf, 1963.

Wetmore, Alexander, and other eminent ornithologists. *Song and Garden Birds of North America.* Washington, D.C.: National Geographic Society, 1964.

The Life and
Adventures of
John Nicol,
Mariner

The Life and Adventures of John Nicol, Mariner

Edited and with an Introduction
by Tim Flannery

Atlantic Monthly Press
New York

Introduction and the editing in this edition copyright © 1997 by Tim Flannery

The author gratefully acknowledges Edward Stanley for his advice on naval history.

First published in 1822
Published in 1997 by The Text Publishing Company, Melbourne, Australia
Printed in the United States of America

FIRST AMERICAN EDITION

Library of Congress Cataloging-in-Publication Data

Nicol, John, 1755–1825.
   [Life and adventures, 1776–1801]
   The life and adventures of John Nicol, mariner / edited and
introduced by Tim Flannery.
      p.   cm.
   Originally published. Life and adventures, 1776–1801. Melbourne,
Vic. : Text. Pub., 1997.
   Includes index.
   ISBN 0-87113-755-0
   1. Nicol, John, 1755–1825—Journeys. 2. Voyages and travels.
3. United States—History—Revolution—Personal narratives—British.
I. Flannery, Tim F. (Tim Fridtjof), 1956–   . II. Title.
G530.N6   1999
910.4'5—dc21   99-24704

Atlantic Monthly Press
841 Broadway
New York, NY 10003

99 00 01 02   10 9 8 7 6 5 4 3 2 1

Contents

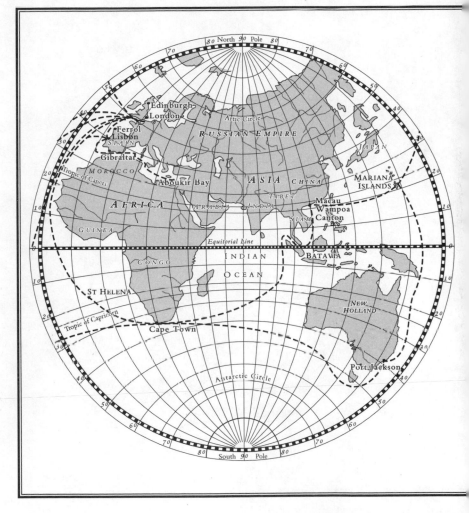

Map of the world as Nicol would have

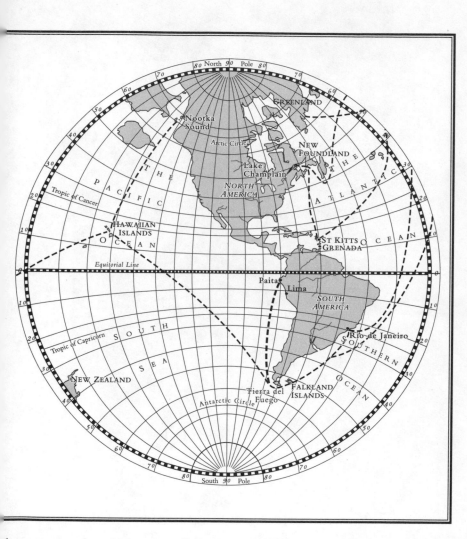

known it, showing some of his journeys.

JOHN NICOL

MARINER, AGE 67

Introduction

by Tim Flannery

J OHN NICOL TWICE circled the globe, in the process visiting all six habitable continents. He fought American revolutionaries and Napoleon's navy, was in Hawaii when Cook's murderers were still young, in Port Jackson when Sydney consisted of about a thousand souls, and in the West Indies when African slaves were beginning to experiment with the music which would become blues and jazz. In short, as he roamed the world in the late eighteenth century, he saw the modern age in its infancy.

The world John Nicol records is not one of admirals, governors and high officials, for he was by his own admission a simple 'bungs'—an 'unlettered' cooper. He describes a world seen from below decks; a world peopled by slaves, convicts and Chinese barbers, many of whom Nicol counted among his friends. As such, his story is an extreme rarity. People like Nicol usually lacked the means to have their adventures recorded, and publishers were largely uninterested in such autobiographies. Indeed, a significant fraction of Nicol's compatriots would not

even have lived to tell their stories. When he sailed, mortality rates of 15 per cent *per annum* were not looked upon as especially bad, yet Nicol survived twenty-five years at sea.[1]

The story of how this book came into existence is almost as remarkable as the one Nicol himself tells. Picture yourself in a street in Edinburgh with the freezing winter of 1822 just beginning to relax its grip. An old derelict totters feebly along, picking tiny fragments of coal from between the icy cobbles. These he places in the pocket of an old apron tied round his waist. They will be used to light a small fire, over which he will crouch, trying to fight off the chill. As he searches for his coals, the old man is approached by a 'very strange person' and so begins the encounter which, after a long and happenstance history, places this book in your hands today.[2]

The 'very strange person' was John Howell, who was to record and edit Nicol's work. Even in nineteenth-century Scotland Howell was an anomaly. He described himself as a 'polyartist'. Although a bookbinder by trade, he was an inveterate inventor and tinkerer by nature. The most enduring of his contrivances is the 'plough', a device used by bookbinders

---

1 Simmons, J. J. (III), 'Those Vulgar Tubes', *Studies in Nautical Archaeology* no. 1, Department of Archaeology, Texas University, 1991.
2 Nicol, John, *The Life and Adventures of John Nicol, Mariner, with a foreword and afterword by Alexander Laing*, Cassell & Company, London, 1937, 27.

well into the present century. Alexander Laing, who gave some biographical notes on Howell, remarked of this invention that 'many a careless binder has ruined good books by too exuberant cropping [with it].'[1]

Howell's other inventions included 'a reliable salve for the ringworm' and a method for the fabrication of false teeth. Transport also intrigued him. He invented a flying machine (the testing of which, from the roof of an old tannery, cost him a broken leg), and a sort of prototype submarine. This latter nearly led to fratricide, for John encouraged an unwilling brother to enter the 'large model of a fish' for its test run on the River Leith. The brother refused, however, and John took his place. A contemporary account reports that:

> Scarcely had the fish entered the water when it capsized: the keel turning upwards, and poor John was submerged. Sounds of an alarming kind were heard to issue from the belly of the fish, and no time was lost in dragging it to the bank, when the inventor was liberated from his perilous position; but it took nearly half an hour before 'suspended animation' was fully restored.[2]

Howell's other great interest lay in the exploits of military men and adventurers. He published five books, three of which concerned such people. The first, *Journal of a Soldier of the 71st, or Glasgow Regiment* was followed by *The Life and Adventures of John Nicol, Mariner* and,

1 *Life and Adventures*, 1937, 26.
2 ibid., 28.

3

finally, *The Life of Alexander Alexander Written by Himself.* Howell's method seems to have consisted of befriending old soldiers and sailors, then spending months writing down or editing their life stories. One wonders whether they moved into his house for the duration. Whatever the case, Howell's motives were noble ones, for he signed over royalties to his adoptees, and endeavoured to use their stories to obtain for them their well deserved pensions.

Howell's 1822 edition of *The Life and Adventures of John Nicol, Mariner* is a modest little book, measuring just sixteen centimetres by ten. Its only illustration is a simple drawing of Nicol himself—in all probability placed there to evoke the reader's pity. It shows the weatherbeaten and wistful countenance of one who has seen much of life. The book's rarity now suggests that the print run was small. Its only republication occurred in 1937 when Cassell issued an edition 'embellished with numerous original designs' by Gordon Grant, and with a foreword and afterword by Laing, who claims that *Life and Adventures* is the earliest reminiscence by an ordinary sailor that 'has any claim to permanence as literature'. The book, he says, 'acquainted me ... with a distinct personality I should have felt far the poorer for not having known, and from time to time I have sought him out again, in his book, with the same pleasure I should take in looking up an old friend.'

John Nicol had 'seen more of the world than most persons in Edinburgh, perhaps in Britain' according

to Howell, yet throughout his life he seems to have remained almost unworldly. This may stem from the fact that, like many seamen, he led a largely sheltered life. While at sea, his domestic and financial arrangements were made for him. Decisions were made by others, and there was little time for romance with all its complications. In these ways, going to sea was akin to joining a religious order.

Nicol was not a sailor of the rum, sodomy and the lash school. When he first went to sea he read his Bible daily and it troubled his conscience that he lost the habit. He was shy, did not drink heavily and was appalled by foul language. At times one wonders how this good and simple man mixed it with the recurrent brutality of life at sea.

Nicol's naivety shows through nowhere more clearly than in his first romance. After meeting a young woman on a coach journey he feels 'something uncommon arise in [his] breast'. After a number of efforts, he 'summonsed the resolution to take her hand in mine; I pressed it gently, she drew faintly back'. With little more encouragement than that, Nicol decides upon marriage and, were it not for a recalcitrant prospective father-in-law, may have succeeded in his designs. He was equally 'at sea' with the most important female in his life, a convict girl named Sarah Whitlam who became his great love. Yet time has shown that his assessment of Sarah Whitlam was hardly an accurate one.

Given the editorial role Howell played, one

wonders how much of *The Life and Adventures of John Nicol, Mariner* represents his input, for the beauty of the language sometimes makes the reader doubt whether it could be the work of an unlettered cooper. Laing speculates that Howell's influence on the book's style and content was minor. He notes that the two works published by Howell alone (*An Essay upon the War Galleys of the Ancients* and *The Life and Adventures of Alexander Selkirk*) 'lack the passages of terse grandeur which lifts Nicol's story, from time to time, to the level of great English prose'.[1] Howell was also a great respecter of facts, and is unlikely to have tampered with the subjects of Nicol's work. Nicol himself says that he will make his story as interesting as is in his power, 'consistent with truth'; its detail is in itself a guide to its authenticity. He remembers, for instance, how Chinese washer women kept a pig in 'a cage-like box fixed to the stern of their sampan.' On the Falkland Islands the geese he saw were 'very pretty, spreckled like a partridge.'

There is something very special about Nicol's prose, with its attention to minute detail, recalled decades after the events occurred. Perhaps this derives from Nicol's style, which is clearly in the great oral storytelling tradition of the sea, owing more to the long tradition of the storytelling bards than to the written prose of his contemporaries. The natural

1 *Life and Adventures*, 1937, 23.

rhythm and pattern of such language is a powerful aid to memory. The stories, told over and over, become ever more refined and compelling. Nicol even draws a picture of himself as raconteur, late in his life, when he takes a boat to London to attempt to gain his pension: 'I was at sea again ... I had always a crowd round me listening to my accounts of the former voyages that I had made ... I was very happy.' From such stories has come this vivid and romantic tale of travel to the hidden corners of the world.

A large part of the fascination of Nicol's book lies in his service as steward aboard the *Lady Juliana* transport which, as part of the second fleet, brought over two hundred female convicts to Australia in 1790. The logbook of the *Lady Juliana* is long lost, so Nicol's account is the main source of information for the voyage.[1] His time aboard the *Lady Juliana* (which he recollects as the *Lady Julian*) was formative, for Nicol fell in love with a convict girl named Sarah Whitlam. She was his first real love, and Nicol 'courted her for a week and upwards, and would have married her on the spot had there been a clergyman on board'. She was, he said, 'as kind and true a creature as ever lived'. Before the voyage was out she bore him a son, John.

On the evening of 3 June 1790 the *Lady Juliana*

---

1 Flynn, Michael, *The Second Fleet: Britain's Grim Convict Armada of 1790*, Library of Australian History, Sydney, 1993, 1–8.

entered Port Jackson after almost a year at sea. Nicol
records how the landing was 'almost to our sorrow'.
He knew his time with Sarah was running out. But it
was a special moment, for that evening John Nicol
and Watkin Tench—the great chronicler of the birth
of European Australia, who had rowed out to meet
the ship amid squalls and cloudbursts—stood together
under the one set of sails. For Tench the arrival of
the *Lady Juliana* was a moment of exquisite joy. 'News
burst upon us like meridian splendour on a blind
man,' he records as he learned for the first time of the
French Revolution, the madness of George III and the
loss of the *Guardian* supply ship. Nicol, characteristi-
cally, gives us a glimpse of an intensely human story
inside this great historic moment. He doesn't care
about revolutions, kings or shipwrecks. His thoughts
are all about his imminent separation from his new
family.

Nicol spent six weeks in Port Jackson with his
beloved Sarah and their infant son. They were,
perhaps, the happiest days of his life. Although his
recollections of Port Jackson were thirty years old by
the time they were written down, they are remarkably
accurate. He records, for instance that there were only
two 'natives' in the town at that time. They were
Abaroo and Nanbaree, survivors of the smallpox epidemic who were then living with Surgeon White
(Nanbaree) and the Reverend and Mrs Johnson
(Abaroo). He also records some curious attributes of
the 'sweet tea' which was drunk with such avidity by

the first fleeters. Nicol wrote that 'it is infused and drank like the China tea. I liked it much. It requires no sugar and is both a bitter and a sweet'. He also regarded its medicinal qualities highly:

> There was an old female convict, her hair quite grey with age, her face shrivelled, who was suckling a child she had borne in the colony. Everyone went to see her, and I among the rest. It was a strange sight. Her hair was quite white. Her fecundity was ascribed to the sweet tea.

Tench and others tell us of this woman, but none do so with the descriptive vividness of Nicol. And none ascribe her fecundity to the tea!

As the hour of his departure approached, Nicol became desperate to stay with his wife and child. He was, however, contracted to return to England and the ship was short of hands. He relates that:

> It was not without the aid of the military we were brought on board. I offered to lose my wages but we were short of hands . . . The captain could not spare a man and requested the aid of the governor. I thus was forced to leave Sarah, but we exchanged faith. She promised to remain true.

Nicol spent the next few years trying to return to Port Jackson, but without success. While thus engaged, he heard from a runaway convict that Sarah had left the colony for Bombay. Nicol did not know what to make of this information, and nor do I. Sarah

did not sail for Bombay until 1796, yet Nicol claims to have heard of it in 1791-92.[1] Was Sarah sending out misinformation, or had Nicol misremembered? Given his subsequent sailing schedule, the latter seems unlikely, for after 1794 Nicol was fighting in the French Revolutionary wars. Nicol visited Sarah's parents in Lincoln, but they could tell him nothing. Hoping for the best yet fearing betrayal, he tried to get a passage to Bombay, but could not find a berth, even as a paying passenger. In all his subsequent journeying, the possibility of being reunited with Sarah is continually on his mind. 'She was,' he says, 'still the idol of all my affections.'

In 1801 Nicol returned to his native Edinburgh, being 'too old to undertake any more love pilgrimages after an individual, as I knew not in what quarter of the globe she was, or whether she were dead or alive'. But what of Sarah and her son? The children of convicts were often removed from their parents, and little John's fate is not recorded. Sarah, in contrast, first appears in the records of the colony the day after Nicol's tearful departure, but the telling of that story must await its proper place.

Nicol's Australian interlude occupied a fraction of his twenty-five years at sea. Much of what he records elsewhere is of great interest to the contemporary reader, for he recalls events and cultures which were glossed over by his better educated and better

1 *The Second Fleet*, 461.

connected contemporaries. The importance of Nicol's work is magnified by the fact that he was far above the ordinary in his humanity, memory and wit. He also loved a song, and nowhere does this shine through more clearly than during his visit to Jamaica, where he lived for some time among slaves. He says of these poor people, 'I esteemed them in my heart' and they clearly reciprocated.

Nicol records that during his stay, he and the other crew were fed on a 'cut and come again' basis, and he always ensured that he took a little something extra to give to the plantation slaves. They in return invited him to a dance. Nicol was touched to find that these poorest of the poor had purchased some 'three bit maubi' as they called rum. They did not drink this luxury themselves, but bought it on his account, having heard that sailors prefer it. The vibrancy of the songs he heard that night shone on undimmed in Nicol's memory for over three decades:

> I lost my shoe in an old canoe
>   Johnio, come Winum so;
> I lost my boot in a pilot boat,
>   Johnio, come Winum so

and

> My Massa a bad man,
>   My Missis cry honey,
> Is this the damn nigger
>   You buy wi my money?
>   Ting a ring ting, ting a ring ting, tarro

The cruel treatment of the slaves clearly appalled Nicol. He records the beating of a pregnant woman and the part he and a colleague played in terminating it. He talks of a one-legged runaway blacksmith chained to his bench, and a slave forced to wear a barbarous collar of spikes. His anger at these outrages remained, like the songs, unblunted by the years.

Nicol's next voyage was more carefree. His journey in search of discovery and trade aboard the *King George* was to take him to Hawaii just after the murder of James Cook. Indeed, the *King George* was the first ship to arrive in the islands after Cook's discovery of them. Nicol records that:

> Almost every man on board took a native woman for a wife while the vessel remained ... The fattest woman I ever saw in my life our gunner chose for a wife. We were forced to hoist her on board. Her thighs were as thick as my waist. No hammock in the ship would hold her. Many jokes were cracked upon the pair.

He also records the wonderful facility of the Hawaiians to parody the Europeans:

> We had a merry facetious fellow on board called Dickson. He sung pretty well. He squinted and the natives mimicked him. Abenoue, King of Atooi, could cock his eye like Dickson better than any of his subjects. Abenoue called him Billicany, from his often singing 'Rule Britannia' ... Abenoue loved him better than any man in the ship, and always

embraced him every time they met on shore or in the ship, and began to sing, 'Tule Billicany, Billicany tule,' etc.

Then comes Nootka Sound, the Marianas, and finally back to Nicol's beloved Wampoa in China, which he visited three times. How can we believe that Nicol was befriended there by a Chinaman named Tommy Linn, a barber-surgeon who contracted to shave the entire crew of Nicol's ship during the duration of their stay? Nicol was really at home among the Chinese, and he was accepted into their bosom when he saved a child from drowning.

The current was strong and the boy was carried down with rapidity. I leapt into the river and saved him with great difficulty . . . and soon had the pleasure of delivering him to his father who stood on the beach wringing his hands.

I wished to go on board, but the Chinese would have me to his house where I was most kindly received and got my dinner in great style. I like their manner of setting out the table at dinner. All that is to be eaten is placed upon the table at once, and all the liquors at the same time. You have all before you and you may make your choice.

He also records, in a delightful manner, some examples of the lingua franca used between Chinese and European traders. Here were the antecedents of the diverse modern pidgins of Oceania, some of which are now the national languages of Pacific nations:

Tommy Linn the barber ... was a walking newspaper. His first word every morning was, 'Hey, yaw,
what fashion?' and we used the same phrase to him.
One morning he came, and the first thing he said
was, 'Hey, yaw, what fashion? Soldier man's ship
come to Lingcome bar.' We, after a few hours, heard
that a man-of-war frigate had arrived ...

They are much alarmed at the appearance of a
man-of-war ship, and they often say, 'Englishman
too much cruel, too much fight.' There were some
English seamen flogged for mutiny while we lay in
the river. The Chinese wept like children for the
men, saying, 'Hey, yaw, Englishman too much cruel,
too much flog, too much flog.'

Nicol's final service was aboard a series of ships
fighting in the French Revolutionary Wars. Nicol's
ship the *Goliah* participated in the Battle of the Nile,
one of Nelson's three great victories, and one of the
most celebrated naval victories of all time. What is
surprising is the presence of women and the role they
played in the battle. Nicol writes:

The women behaved as well as the men, and got
a present for their bravery from the grand
signior ... I was much indebted to the gunner's
wife who gave her husband and me a drink of wine
every now and then which lessened our fatigue
much. There were some of the women wounded,
and one woman belonging to Leith died of her
wounds and was buried on a small island in the

bay. One woman bore a son in the heat of the action.

What a birth that must have been! After the guns ceased their booming, Nicol records what 'an awful sight it was. The whole bay was covered with dead bodies, mangled, wounded and scorched'. This carnage had been caused when the French war ship *L'Orient* blew up close to Nicol's *Goliath*. Such an event was rare in the naval warfare of the day.

At the termination of his service Nicol returned to Edinburgh, where he married his cousin Margaret. It was probably a match based more on affection and convenience than love. He had saved a relatively large sum (which was apparently kept sewn in his clothes) from his decades at sea, and this enabled him to set up a prosperous cooperage business. He also purchased a small cottage and for a time enjoyed married life. But then war (the Napoleonic Wars) broke out again, and the press gangs began their ghastly rounds. These gangs were sanctioned to kidnap and sell into forced labour any sailor they could find. *— HOW IS IT DIFFERENT*

It is hard for us, in our egalitarian age, to understand *FROM THE* just what a threat the press gangs represented to *MILITARY* someone such as Nicol. The most vivid description of *DRAFT TO* their rapacity comes from Admiral Anson's *Voyage* *WHICH SO* *Around the World.*[1] Although it was written sixty years *MANY OF US* *FELL PREY?*

1 Walter, R., *A Voyage Round the World in the Years 1740, 1, 2, 3, 4 by George Anson, Esq.*, Alex Lawrie & Co., Edinburgh, 1741, 1804, 20.

earlier, little had changed by Nicol's time. The various efforts made to obtain marines for Anson all failed until:

> five hundred invalids [were] to be collected from the out pensioners of Chelsea college ... who, from their age, wounds, or other infirmities, are incapable of service in marching regiments ... But instead of five hundred, there came on board no more than two hundred and fifty nine; for all those who had limbs and strength to walk out of Portsmouth, deserted, leaving behind them only such as were literally invalids, most of them being sixty years of age, and some of them upwards of seventy.

This 'aged and diseased detachment' was destined to undertake a five-year-long voyage around the world, which was almost unequalled in its arduousness. They dropped like flies. The wounds some had received over fifty years before broke open afresh due to the scurvy. Few survived to see action, much less their homeland.

And so we find John Nicol, newly married at the age of forty-six, unable to sleep in his own bed for fear of being pressed. For eleven years he was forced to live the life of a fugitive in rural Scotland. Yet he remained loyal to king and country, and upon hearing the news of the victory at Trafalgar recalled:

> None but an old tar can feel the joy I felt. I wrought none the next day but walked about enjoying the feeling of triumph. Every now and then I felt the greatest desire to hurra aloud, and many an hurra my heart gave that my mouth uttered not.

To 'hurra' of course, would have alerted the press gangs to his being 'an old tar'.

Finally, at the age of fifty-eight, Nicol felt that it was safe to return home. His homecoming was a joyous one. Perhaps the excitement was too much for Margaret, his wife, for she did not long outlive it. Her death brought on another trial, for Nicol discovered that for years there had been 'more money going out than I by my industry could bring in . . . and a number of debits . . . had been contracted unknown to me'.

Nicol travelled to London in search of the pension he desperately needed and richly deserved. His fate in this endeavour would be familiar to anyone who has been shunted from one part of the bureaucracy to another. First he learned that his old friend Captain Portlock, who could have provided a testimonial of his service, had died six weeks earlier. He then went to Somerset House to gain a certificate of service. A clerk there sent him to Admiralty House where another clerk told him he had waited too long before applying. As a last ditch effort to gain the all-important certificate he went to see the governor of Greenwich Hospital, but he was on holiday in Scotland. Broke, Nicol returned to Edinburgh.

And so, in the early spring of 1822, at the age of sixty-seven, this fine old sailor was forced to walk the streets of his city, seeking fragments of coal to prevent himself from dying of cold. Had he not met John Howell he would have died in anonymity.

It is heartwarming to know that Howell's charity

really did make a difference to Nicol, for unlike so many of his fellows, he 'died like an admiral, in bed, having evenly rounded out his threescore years and ten'.[1] His funds were not exhausted even then, for a sum of 30 pounds was left to his relatives.

As great as Howell's gift was to Nicol, he left the world a far greater one, for Nicol's recollections offer a unique glimpse of an extraordinary world as it was seen through the eyes of a simple yet most acute watcher upon life. Nicol's tale still has the power to inspire us to adventure, and surely his prayers still go with those who love travel:

> Old as I am, my heart is still unchanged; and were I young and stout as I have been, again would I sail upon discovery—but, weak and stiff, I can only send my prayers with the tight ship and her merry hearts.

*

I have used the text of the original edition of *The Life and Adventures of John Nicol, Mariner*, published by William Blackwood in Edinburgh in 1822. I have modernised Nicol's spelling and punctuation, cor rected the occasional error and added some footnotes, marked by an asterisk (*). Nicol's own notes are marked by a dagger (†).

1 *Life and Adventures*, 1937, 25.

A Most Interesting Character
by John Howell

EARLY IN THE spring of the year 1822 John Nicol, the narrator of these adventures, was pointed out to me as a most interesting character, and one who had seen more of the world than most persons in Edinburgh, perhaps in Britain.

He was walking feebly along with an old apron tied round his waist, in which he carried a few very small pieces of coal he had picked up in his wanderings through the streets. From the history I had got of his adventures, I felt grieved to see the poor old man. I requested him to call at my shop. He came in the evening. After a little conversation with him I was astonished at the information he possessed, and the spirit that awoke in the old tar.

I had no interest by which to serve myself. Money I had not to give. As the only means of being of permanent use to him, and perhaps of obtaining the pension he is by service entitled to, I thought of taking down a narrative of his life, from his own mouth. This

I have done, as nearly as I could, in his own words.

Even in the midst of all his present wants, he is a contented cheerful old man of sober habits, and bears an excellent character from those people who have employed him in his trade as a cooper. I have conversed with one of his shipmates who was with him in the *Edgar*, *Goliah* and *Ramilies*, who informs me he was as sober and steady a man as ever sailed.

I have never met with one possessed of a more tenacious memory or who gave a more distinct account of any occurrence he had witnessed, of which any gentleman may satisfy himself, as John will wait upon him with pleasure, upon application to the Publisher.

Edinburgh
12th November 1822

1

*Author's Birth—Early Propensities
—He Goes to London—Is
Apprenticed to a Cooper
—Enters the Navy—Smugglers—
Arrives at Quebec.*

Preface

T O THE PUBLIC it must appear strange that an unlettered individual, at the advanced age of sixty-seven years, should sit down to give them a narrative of his life. Imperious circumstances must plead my excuse. Necessity, even more than the importunity of well-wishers, at length compels me. I shall use my humble endeavour to make it as interesting as is in my power, consistent with truth.

My life, for a period of twenty five years, was a continued succession of change. Twice I circumnavigated the globe; three times I was in China, twice in Egypt, and more than once sailed along the whole landboard of America from Nootka Sound to Cape Horn. Twice I doubled it—but I will not anticipate the events I am about to narrate.

Old as I am, my heart is still unchanged; and were I young and stout as I have been, again would I sail upon discovery—but, weak and stiff, I can only send my prayers with the tight ship and her merry hearts.

John Nicol

I WAS BORN in the small village of Currie, about six miles from Edinburgh, in the year 1755. The first wish I ever formed was to wander, and many a search I gave my parents in gratifying my youthful passion.

My mother died in child-bed when I was very young, leaving my father in charge of five children. Two died young and three came to man's estate. My oldest brother died of his wounds in the West Indies, a lieutenant in the navy. My younger brother went to America and I have never heard from him. Those trifling circumstances I would not mention, were I not conscious that the history of the dispersion of my father's family is the parallel of thousands of the families of my father's rank in Scotland.

My father, a cooper to trade, was a man of talent and information, and made it his study to give his children an education suited to their rank in life; but my unsteady propensities did not allow me to make the most of the schooling I got. I had read *Robinson Crusoe* many times over and longed to be at sea. We had been living for some time in Borrowstownness. Every moment I could spare was spent in the boats or about the shore.

When I was about fourteen years of age my father was engaged to go to London to take a small charge in a chemical work. Even now I recollect the transports my young mind felt when my father informed me I was to go to London. I counted the hours and minutes to the moment we sailed on board the

Glasgow and Paisley Packet, Captain Thompson master. There were a sergeant and a number of recruits, a female passenger, my father, brother and self, besides the crew. It was in the month of December we sailed, and the weather was very bad. All the passengers were seasick; I never was.

This was in the year 1769, when the dreadful loss was sustained on the coast of Yorkshire—above thirty sail of merchantmen were wrecked. We were taken in the same gale but rode it out. Next morning we could hardly proceed for wreck, and the whole beach was covered. The country people were collecting and driving away the dead bodies in wagons.

My father embraced this opportunity to prejudice me against being a sailor. He was a kind but strict parent and we dared not disobey him. The storm had made no impression upon my mind sufficient to alter my determination. My youthful mind could not separate the life of a sailor from dangers and storms, and I looked upon them as an interesting part of the adventures I panted after. I had been on deck all the time and was fully occupied in planning the means of escape. I enjoyed the voyage much, was anxious to learn everything, and was a great favourite with the captain and crew.

One of my father's masters was translating a French work on chemistry. I went to the printing office with the proofs almost every day. Once, in passing near the Tower, I saw a dead monkey floating

in the river. I had not seen above two or three in my life. I thought it of great value.

I stripped at once and swam in for it. An English boy, who wished it likewise but who either would or could not swim, seized it when I landed, saying 'he would fight me for it'. We were much of a size. Had there been a greater difference, I was not of a temper to be easily wronged—so I gave him battle. A crowd gathered and formed a ring. Stranger as I was, I got fair play. After a severe contest, I came off victor. The English boy shook hands, and said, 'Scotchman, you have won it.'

I had fought naked as I came out of the water, so I put on my clothes and carried off the prize in triumph—came home and got a beating from my father for fighting and staying my message; but the monkey's skin repaid me for all my vexations.

I remained in London scarcely twelve months when my father sent me to Scotland to learn my trade. I chose the profession of a cooper to please my father. I was for some time with a friend at the Queensferry but, not agreeing with him, I served out my tedious term of apprenticeship at Borrowstownness. My heart was never with the business. While my hands were hooping barrels my mind was at sea and my imagination in foreign climes.

Soon as my period of bondage expired I bade my friends farewell and set out to Leith with a merry heart; and, after working journeyman a few months, to enable me to be a proficient in my trade, I entered

on board the *Kent's Regard*, commanded by Lieutenant Ralph Dundas. She was the tender at this time (1776) stationed in Leith Roads.

Now I was happy, for I was at sea. To me the order to weigh anchor and sail for the Nore was the sound of joy.* My spirits were up at the near prospect of obtaining the pleasures I had sighed for since the first dawn of reason. To others it was the sound of woe, the order that cut off the last faint hope of escape from a fate they had been impressed into much against their inclination and interest. I was surprised to see so few who, like myself, had chosen it for the love of that line of life. Some had been forced into it by their own irregular conduct but the greater number were impressed men.**

Ogilvie's revenue cutter and the *Hazard* sloop of war had a short time before surprised a smuggling cutter delivering her cargo in St Andrew's Bay. The smuggler fought them both until all her ammunition was spent, and resisted their boarding her until the very last by every means in their power. A good many of the king's men were wounded, and not a few of the smugglers. When taken possession of they declared the captain had been killed in the action and thrown overboard. The remainder were marched to Edinburgh Castle and kept there until the evening before

---

* The Nore: a lighthouse near Hastings on the south-east coast of England.
** These were men who had been kidnapped by press gangs and forced into naval service.

we sailed. When they came on board we were all struck with their stout appearance and desperate looks; a set of more resolute fellows I have never in my life met with. They were all sent down to the press-room. The volunteers were allowed to walk the decks and had the freedom of the ship.

One night, on our voyage to the Nore, the whole ship was alarmed by loud cries of murder from the press-room. An armed force was sent down to know the cause and quell the riot. They arrived just in time to rescue, with barely the life, from the hands of these desperadoes, a luckless wretch who had been an informer for a long time in Leith. A good many in the press-room were indebted to him for their present situation.

The smugglers had learned from them what he was and with one accord had fallen upon him and beat him in a dreadful manner. When he was brought to the surgeon's berth there were a number of severe cuts upon his person. From his disgraceful occupation of informer, few on board pitied him. After a few days he got better and was able to walk, but was no more sent down to the press-room.

Upon our arrival at the Nore, a writ of *habeas corpus* was sent on board for one of the smugglers for a debt. We all suspected him to have been the captain, and this a scheme to get him off from being kept on board of a man of war.

I was sent on board the *Proteus*, twenty-gun ship, commanded by Captain Robinson, bound for New

York.* The greater number of the smugglers were put on board the same vessel. They were so stout, active, and experienced seamen that Captain Robinson manned his barge with them.

We sailed from Portsmouth with ordnance stores and 100 men to man the floating batteries upon Lake Champlain.**

I was appointed cooper, which was a great relief to my mind, as I messed with the steward in his room. I was thus away from the crew. I had been much annoyed and rendered very uncomfortable, until now, from the swearing and loose talking of the men in the tender. I had all my life been used to the strictest conversation, prayers night and morning. Now I was in a situation where family worship was unknown and, to add to the disagreeable situation I was in, the troops were unhealthy. We threw overboard every morning a soldier or a sheep.

At first I said my prayers and read my Bible in private, but truth makes me confess I gradually became more and more remiss, and before long I was a sailor like the rest; but my mind felt very uneasy and I made many weak attempts to amend.

We sailed with our convoy direct for Quebec. Upon our arrival the men, having been so long on salt provisions, made too free with the river water and

---

* The American War of Independence had begun.
** Lake Champlain: American Lake bordering New York and Vermont.

were almost all seized with the flux.* The *Proteus* was upon this account laid up for six weeks, during which time the men were in the hospital. After having done the ship's work, Captain Robinson was so kind as allow me to work on shore, where I found employment from a Frenchman who gave me excellent encouragement. I worked on shore all day and slept on board at night.

* The flux: dysentry.

2

Canada—Mode of Fishing—
Serpents—Floats of Wood—Author
Sails to the West Indies—Slavery—
Arrives at Newfoundland.

CANADA IS A fine country. Provisions abound in it and the inhabitants are kind and humane. Salmon abound in the St Lawrence. The Indians come alongside every day with them, either smoked or fresh, which they exchange for biscuit or pork. They take them in wicker baskets wrought upon stakes stuck into the sand within the tide mark. The baskets have two entrances, one pointing up the river, the other pointing down. The entrances have no doors, but sharp-pointed wands prevent the exit of the fish or their returning: if once the head is entered the whole body must follow. They resemble in this the wire mouse trap used in Britain. Some have shutting doors, as in Scotland, that swing with the tide. When it is back, the Indians examine their baskets, and seldom find them without more or less fish.

The French eat many kinds of the serpents that abound in the country. Whether they are good eating I do not know, as I never could bring myself to taste them. They must be good, as it is not for want of other varieties they are made choice of. I often went of an evening with my master to catch them. We caught them with forked sticks; the Frenchman was very dexterous and I soon learned. We often caught two dozen in an evening. When we perceived one we ran the forks of the stick upon its neck, behind the head, and, holding it up from the ground, beat it upon the head with the other until we dispatched it. When we came home the heads were cut off and the snakes skinned. Their skins were very beautiful and many of

the officers got scabbards made of them for their swords.

I was much surprised at the immense floats of wood that came gliding majestically down the river like floating islands. They were covered with turf, and wood huts upon them, smoke curling from the roofs, and children playing before the doors and the stately matron on her seat, sewing or following her domestic occupations, while the husband sat upon the front with his long pole, guiding it along the banks or from any danger in the river, and their batteau astern to carry them home with the necessaries they procured by the sale of their wood, the produce of their severe winter's labour.*

They had floated thus down the majestic St Lawrence hundreds of miles. It looked like magic and reminded me of the fairies I had often heard of, to see the children sporting and singing in chorus upon these floating masses, the distance diminishing the size of their figures and softening the melody of their voices, while their hardy enterprise astonished the mind upon reflection, and the idea of their enjoyment was dashed at the recollection of their hardships. They really are a cheerful race.

I can think of no pleasure more touching to the feelings and soothing to the mind than to lie upon the green banks and listen to the melodious voices of the

* Batteau: a light, flat-bottomed river boat used widely in Canada.

women of a summer evening as they row along in their batteaux, keeping time to the stroke of the oar. For hours I have lain over the breast-netting, looking and listening to them, unconscious of the lapse of time.

The time I had passed since my entrance into the St Lawrence was very pleasant. In our passage up we had run at an amazing rate—the trees and every object seemed to glide from us with the rapidity of lightning, the wind being fresh and direct. We passed the island of Antecost at a short distance and anchored at the island of Beak where the pilots live. It had an old sergeant, at the time, for governor, Ross his name, who had been with Wolfe at the taking of Quebec.

We then stood up the river, wind and tide serving, and passed next the island of Conder. It appeared a perfect garden. Then the Falls of Morant, the mist rising to the clouds. They appeared to fall from a greater height than the vane of our topmast, and made a dreadful roaring. We last of all made the island of Orleans, a most beautiful place. It is quite near the town and is, like the island of Conder, a perfect garden from end to end.

At length our men were all recovered and the stores landed. I bade farewell to my French master and friends on shore, and sailed for Gaspé Bay. We were joined here by the *Assistance*, fifty-gun ship, commanded by Captain Worth.

All the crew got a handsome treat from Governor O'Hara at the baptism of his family. They were

beautiful children, five in number, the oldest a stately girl. None of them had yet been baptised, and the governor embraced the opportunity of the chaplain of the *Assistance* to have this necessary Christian rite performed, as there was not a clergyman at the station and the children had all been born in the Bay. The contrast between the situation of these children and their parents, and the people in Scotland, at the time, made a deep impression upon my mind; and I can say, at no period of my life had the privileges I had left behind appeared so valuable.

From Gaspe Bay we sailed with convoy for the West Indies. The convoy was loaded with salt fish. The American privateers swarmed around like sharks, watching an opportunity to seize any slow-sailing vessel. We took a few of them and brought the convoy safe to its destination.

While watering at St Kitt's we got free of the smugglers. The manner of their escape is the best comment upon their character. Captain Robinson went ashore in his barge. The crew, as I said before, was composed of them, coxswain and all. Soon after the captain left the water's edge they took to their heels. One of them became faint-hearted after he was away and returned. The others, that very night, while search was making for them, seized a boat belonging to the island and rowed over to St Eustatia, a Dutch neutral island, boarded, overpowered and carried off an American brig, and sold her at one of the French islands. None of them were ever taken that I heard

of. The one that returned never again held up his head, as he was looked down upon by the crew.

While we lay at any of the West Indian islands our decks used to be crowded by the female slaves, who brought us fruit and remained on board all Sunday until Monday morning—poor things! And all to obtain a bellyful of victuals. On Monday morning the Jolly Jumper, as we called him, was on board with his whip; and, if all were not gone, did not spare it upon their backs.

One cruel rascal was flogging one on our deck, who was not very well in her health. He had struck her once as if she had been a post. The poor creature gave a shriek. Some of our men, I knew not which—there were a good many near him—knocked him overboard. He sunk like a stone. The men gave a hurra! One of the female slaves leaped from the boat alongside into the water and saved the tyrant, who, I have no doubt, often enough beat her cruelly.

I was one of the boarders. We were all armed, when required, with a pike to defend our own vessel should the enemy attempt to board; a tomahawk, cutlass and brace of pistols to use in boarding them. I never had occasion to try their use on board the *Proteus*, as the privateers used to strike after a broadside or two.

While we lay at St Kitt's I took the country fever and was carried to the hospital, where I lay for some days; but my youth, and the kindness of my black nurse, triumphed over the terrible malady. When able

to crawl about the hospital, where many came in sick the one day and were carried out the next to be buried, the thoughts of the neglect of my Maker, and the difference in the life I had for some time led from the manner in which I had been trained up in my youth, made me shudder. With tears I promised myself to reform.

I could now see the land-crabs running through the graves of two or three whom I had left stout and full of health. In the West Indies the grave is dug no deeper than just to hold the body, the earth covering it only a few inches, and all is soon consumed by the land-crabs. The black fellows eat them. When I asked them why they eat these loathsome creatures their answer was, 'Why, they eat me.'

I returned on board free from the fever, but very weak. Soon after we took convoy for England, then sailed into Portsmouth harbour and were docked and repaired. While my weakness lasted, my serious impressions remained, but I must again confess: as I became strong in my body, the impressions upon my mind became weak.

As soon as the *Proteus* was repaired we took convoy for St John's, Newfoundland. On this voyage we had very severe weather. Our foremast was carried away and we arrived off St John's in a shattered state, weary and spent with fatigue. To add to our misfortunes we were three weeks lying before the harbour, and could not make it, on account of an island of ice that blocked up its mouth. During these three tedious weeks we never

saw the sun or sky, the fogs were so dense. Had it not been for the incessant blowing of the fishermen's horns to warn each other, and prevent their being run down, we might as well have been in the middle of the ocean in a winter night. The bows of the *Proteus* could not be seen from her quarter-deck. We received supplies and intelligence from the harbour by the fishermen. At length this tedious fog cleared up, and we entered the harbour. The *Proteus*, having been an old East India-man, was now quite unfit for service; and the admiral caused her be made a prison-ship.

After this I was wholly employed on shore, brewing spruce for the fleet.* I had two and often three men under me to cut the spruce and firewood for my use. I was a man of some consequence even with the inhabitants, as I could make a present of a bottle of essence to them. They made presents of rum to me. I thus lived very happy, and on good terms with them.

Nothing surprised me more than the early marriage of the Newfoundland females. They have children at twelve years of age. I had some dealings with a merchant, and dined two or three times at his house. I inquired at him for his daughter, a pretty young woman whom I saw at table the first time. To my astonishment he told me she was his wife and the mother of three fine children.

---

* Spruce: a kind of beer made from spruce (*Picea*) and sugar, and slightly fermented.

In the winter, the cold on the Barrens, as the inhabitants call them, is dreadful. The Barrens are the spaces where there is no wood. Over these we must use our utmost speed to reach the woods. When once there, we are in comparative comfort; it is even warm among the trees. The thoughts of the Barrens again to be crossed is the only damp to our present enjoyment, as we are soon in a sweat from the exercise in cutting the wood.

When the snow first sets in it is necessary to remain at home until the weather clears up. Then the men put on their snow shoes, and three or four abreast thus make a path to the woods. In the middle of the day the sun hardens the path, and along these the wood is dragged upon sledges to the town by dogs. A person, not knowing the cause, would smile to see us urging on our dogs, ourselves pulling with one hand and rubbing our ears with the other. I am certain it would be a cure for tardiness of any kind to be forced to cross the Barrens in winter.

Numbers of the fishermen, who have gambled away their hard-won summer's wages, are forced thus to earn their winter's maintenance. At this time the greater part of the fishers were Irishmen, the wildest characters man can conceive. Gambling and every vice was familiar to them. Their quarrelling and fighting never ceased, and even murders were sometimes perpetrated upon each other. St Patrick's day is a scene of riot and debauchery unequalled in any town in Ireland.

I saw them myself march in line past an unfortunate man who had been killed in one of their feuds,
and each man that passed him gave the inanimate
body a blow, at the same time calling him by a term
of abuse, significant of the party he had belonged to.
It was unsafe to carry anything after nightfall. I have
been attacked and forced to fight my way more than
once. The respectable inhabitants are thus kept under
a sort of bondage to this riotous race.

In the summer I was much annoyed by the mos-
quitos and yellow nippers, a worse fly; for they bite
cruelly. They make such a buzzing and noise at night
I could not close an eye without my mosquito dose,
that is, rum and spruce.

3

Action between the Surprise *and*
Jason —*Anecdotes* —*Miscellaneous*
Occurrences —*Punishment for*
Neglect of Orders —*Author Paid Off.*

I HAD NOW been eighteen months on shore when I was ordered by Admiral Montague on board the *Surprise*, twenty-eight-gun frigate, commanded by Captain Reeves. Her cooper had been killed a few days before in a severe action with an American vessel.

On board the *Surprise* we had a rougher crew than in the *Proteus*; ninety of them were Irishmen, the rest from Scotland and England. We kept cruising about, taking numbers of the America privateers. After a short but severe action we took the *Jason* of Boston, commanded by the famous Captain Manly, who had been commodore in the American service, had been taken prisoner and broke his parole. When Captain Reeves hailed and ordered him to strike, he returned for answer, 'Fire away! I have as many guns as you.' He had heavier metal but fewer men than the *Surprise*. He fought us for a long time.

I was serving powder as busy as I could, the shot and splinters flying in all directions, when I heard the Irishmen call from one of the guns (they fought like devils, and the captain was fond of them on that account), 'Halloo, Bungs, where are you?'*

I looked to their gun and saw the two horns of my study† across its mouth. The next moment it was through the *Jason's* side. The rogues thus disposed of my study, which I had been using just before the

* Bungs: slang name for a cooper.
† anvil.

action commenced and had placed in a secure place, as I thought, out of their reach. 'Bungs for ever!' they shouted when they saw the dreadful hole it made in the *Jason's* side. Bungs was the name they always gave the cooper.

When Captain Manly came on board the *Surprise* to deliver his sword to Captain Reeves, the half of the rim of his hat was shot off. Our captain returned his sword to him again, saying, 'You have had a narrow escape, Manly.'

'I wish to God it had been my head,' he replied.

When we boarded the *Jason*, we found thirty-one cavalry, who had served under General Burgoyne, acting now as marines on board the *Jason*.

A marine of the name of Kennedy, belonging to the *Surprise*, an intelligent lad and well-behaved, was a great favourite with the surgeon. They used to be constantly together reading and acquiring information. They came from the same place, had been at school together and were dear friends. Kennedy's relations were in a respectable line of life. I never learned the cause of his filling his present lowly situation. As it fell out, poor Kennedy was placed sentinel over the spirit-room of the *Jason*. He was, as I have said, an easy kind of lad and had not been long from home.

He allowed the men to carry away the spirits and they were getting fast drunk when the prize-master perceived it. Kennedy was relieved and sent on board the *Surprise*, and next morning put in irons on board

the *Europa*, the admiral's ship, where he was tried by a court-martial and sentenced to be hanged on the fore-yardarm.

His offence, no doubt, was great, for the men would all have been so much the worse of liquor in a short time that the Americans could have recovered the *Jason* with ease. Yet we were all sorry for him, and would have done anything in our power to redeem him from his present melancholy situation. His friend the surgeon was inconsolable and did everything in his power. He drew up a petition to the admiral for pardon, stating his former good behaviour, his youth and good connections, and everything he could think of in his favour—but all would not do.

He was taken to the place of execution, the rope round his neck. The match was lit, the clergyman at his post. We were all aloft and upon deck to see him run up to the yardarm amidst the smoke of the gun, the signal of death.

When everyone looked for the command to fire, the admiral was pleased to pardon him. He was sent on board the *Surprise* more like a corpse than a living man. He could scarce walk and seemed indifferent to everything on board, as if he knew not whether he was dead or alive. He continued thus for a long time, scarce speaking to anyone. He was free and did no duty, and was the same on board as a passenger.

When the *Surprise* was in port Captain Reeves allowed a degree of licence to his men, but was a strict disciplinarian at sea, punishing the smallest fault. As

we lay in the harbour after the capture of Captain
Manly we got some prize money, and the crew were
very merry. I, as cooper, was down in the steward's
berth. (It was my duty as cooper to serve out the water
and provisions at the regular times.) All my duty at
the time was over and I was in my berth along with
the steward, enjoying ourselves, when a noise and
tumult on board roused us.

We were not touched with liquor; drunkenness was
a vice I never was addicted to. We came upon deck.
The crew were all fighting through amongst each
other in their drink, English against Irish, the officers
mostly on shore, and those on board looking on. I
meant to take no share in the quarrel, when an Irishman came staggering up, crying, 'Erin go bragh!' and
made a blow at me.

My Scottish blood rose in a moment at this prov-
ocation and I was as throng as the rest. How it ended
I hardly recollect. I got a blow that stupefied me, and
all was quiet when I came to myself, the liquor having
evaporated from the others, and the passion from me.

Soon after this we hailed an American privateer
commanded by a Captain Revel, and she struck. He
was a different character from the gallant Manly. The
weather was so foul and the sea ran so high, we could
not send our boat on board, neither could theirs come
on board of us. Captain Reeves ordered her under our
quarter. As he sailed alongside, the weather still very
stormy and night coming on, we were hailed by voices
calling to us, scarcely to be distinguished in the

rattling of our rigging and the howling of the blast. At length we made out with difficulty, that the American captain was going to make some prisoners he had walk overboard.

Captain Reeves, in great anger, ordered the privateer to place a light on her maintop—instead of which he placed one on a float and cast it adrift. The voices again hailed and let us know what had been done. Captain Reeves called to the American that he would sink her in a moment if he did not do as desired and come close under our lee. Towards morning the weather moderated, and we brought Revel and his prisoners on board the *Surprise*. He was a coarse, ill-looking fellow. His treatment of the prisoners made his own treatment the worse: while Manly dined every day at the captain's table, Revel messed by himself or where he chose with the prisoners.

We took convoy for Lisbon, thence to England where we brought Manly and Revel to be detained during the war in Mill Prison. Revel made his escape from the sergeant of marines on his way to the prison, for which the sergeant was tried by a court-martial and sentenced to be hanged, but was afterwards pardoned. It was nothing uncommon for us to take the same men prisoners once or twice in the same season.

We again took convoy for St John's. In the fleet was a vessel called the *Ark* commanded by Captain Noah. She was an armed transport. This we called *Noah's Ark*. In our voyage out an American privateer, equal in weight of metal but having forty-five men

(the *Ark* only sixteen), bore down upon her. The gallant Noah, in his *Ark*, gave battle, we looking on, and after a sharp contest took the American and brought her alongside, her captain lying dead upon her deck. Captain Reeves, with consent of the crew, gave the prize to Noah, who carried her in triumph to Halifax and sold her.

One of our men was whipped through the fleet for stealing some dollars from a merchant ship he was assisting to bring into port. It was a dreadful sight: the unfortunate sufferer tied down on the boat and rowed from ship to ship, getting an equal number of lashes at the side of each vessel from a fresh man. The poor wretch, to deaden his sufferings, had drunk a whole bottle of rum a little before the time of punishment. When he had only two portions to get of his punishment, the captain of the ship perceived he was tipsy and immediately ordered the rest of the punishment to be delayed until he was sober. He was rowed back to the *Surprise*, his back swelled like a pillow, black and blue. Some sheets of thick blue paper were steeped in vinegar and laid to his back. Before he seemed insensible. Now his shrieks rent the air. When better he was sent to the ship, where his tortures were stopped and again renewed.

During the remainder of the war, our duty was the same, taking convoy and capturing American privateers. We came to England with convoy and were docked, then had a cruise in the Channel where we took the *Duke de Chartres*, eighteen-gun ship, and

were ourselves chased into Monts Bay on the coast of Cornwall by a French sixty-four. We ran close inshore and were covered by the old fort which, I believe, had not fired a ball since before the time of Oliver Cromwell—but it did its duty nobly, all night the Frenchman keeping up his fire, the fort and *Surprise* returning it. When day dawned he sheered off, and we only suffered a little in our rigging. The only blood that was shed on our side was an old fogie of the fort who was shot by his own gun.

Quite weary of the monotonous convoy duty and having seen all I could see, I often sighed for the verdant banks of the Forth. At length my wishes were gratified by the return of peace. The *Surprise* was paid off in the month of March 1783. When Captain Reeves came ashore, he completely loaded the long-boat with flags he had taken from the enemy. When one of the officers inquired what he would do with them, he said, laughing, 'I will hang one upon every tree in my father's garden.'

4

Author Arrives in Scotland—
Singular Adventure—He Returns to
London—Enters a Greenland Ship—
Whale Fishery.

I NO SOONER had the money that was due me in my hat than I set off for London direct and, after a few days of enjoyment, put my bedding and chest on board a vessel bound for Leith. Every halfpenny I had saved was in it but nine guineas, which I kept upon my person to provide for squalls. The trader fell down the river but, there being no wind and the tide failing, the captain told us we might sleep in London, only to be sure to be on board before eight o'clock in the morning. I embraced the opportunity and lost my passage.

As all my savings were in my chest, and a number of passengers on board whom I did not like, I immediately took the diligence to Newcastle.* There were no mails running direct for Edinburgh every day, as now. It was the month of March, yet there was a great deal of snow on the ground; the weather was severe, but not so cold as at St John's.

When the diligence set off there were four passengers: two ladies, another sailor and myself. Our lady companions, for the first few stages, were proud and distant, scarcely taking any notice of us. I was restrained by their manner. My companion was quite at home chatting to them, unmindful of their monosyllabic answers. He had a good voice and sung snatches of sea songs, and was unceasing in his endeavours to please. By degrees their reserve wore off and the conversation became general. I now

* Diligence: public stage coach.

learned they were sisters who had been on a visit to a relation in London and were now returning to their father, who was a wealthy farmer.

Before it grew dark we were all as intimate as if we had sailed for years in the same ship. The oldest, who appeared to be about twenty, attached herself to me and listened to my accounts of the different places I had been in with great interest. The youngest was as much interested by my volatile companion.

I felt a something uncommon arise in my breast as we sat side by side. I could think of nothing but my pretty companion. My attentions were not disagreeable to her and I began to think of settling, and how happy I might be with such a wife.

After a number of efforts I summoned resolution to take her hand in mine. I pressed it gently. She drew it faintly back. I sighed. She laid her hand upon my arm, and in a whisper inquired if I was unwell. I was upon the point of telling her what I felt, and my wishes, when the diligence stopped at the inn.

I wished we had been sailing in the middle of the Atlantic, for a covered cart drove up and a stout hearty old man welcomed them by their names, bestowing a hearty kiss upon each. I felt quite disappointed. He was their father. My pretty Mary did not seem to be so rejoiced at her father's kind salutation as might have been expected.

My companion, who was an Englishman, told me he would proceed no farther, but endeavour to win the hand of his pretty partner. I told him my present

situation, that my chest and all I had was on board the Leith trader, and no direction upon it. On this account I was forced to proceed as fast as possible or I would have remained and shared his fortunes with all my heart. I took leave of them with a heavy heart, resolving to return. I could perceive Mary turn pale as I bade her farewell, while her sister looked joy itself when Williams told them he was to proceed no farther. Before the coach set off, I made him promise to write me an account of his success, and that I would return as soon as I had secured my chest and seen my father. He promised to do this faithfully.

I whispered Mary a promise to see her soon, and pressed her hand as we parted. She returned the pressure. I did not feel without hope. When the farmer drove off, Williams accompanying them, I only wished myself in his place.

When the coach reached Newcastle, I soon procured another conveyance to Edinburgh and was at Leith before the vessel. When she arrived I went on board and found all safe. I then went to Borrowstownness, but found my father had been dead for some time.

This was a great disappointment and grief to me. I wished I had been at home to have received his last blessing and advice, but there was no help. He died full of years; and that I may be as well prepared when I shall be called hence is my earnest wish. After visiting his grave and spending a few days with my friends, I became uneasy at not hearing from

Williams. I waited for three weeks; then, losing all patience, I set off myself to see how the land lay. I took leave of home once more, with a good deal of money in my pocket, as I had been almost a miser at home, keeping all for the marriage, should I succeed.

The spring was now advancing apace, when I took my passage in a Newcastle trader and arrived safe at the inn where I had last parted from Mary. It was night when I arrived and, being weary, soon went to bed. I was up betimes in the morning. When I met Williams, he was looking very dull. I shook hands, and asked, 'What cheer?'

He shook his head, and said, 'Why, Jack, we are on the wrong tack, and I fear will never make port. I had no good news to send, so it was of no use to write. I was at the farmer's last night. He swears, if ever I come near his house again, he will have me before the justice as an idle vagrant. My fair jilt is not much concerned, and I can scarce get a sight of her. She seems to shun me.'

I felt a chillness come over me at this information, and asked him what he meant to do.

'Why, set sail this day. Go to my mother, give her what I can spare, and then to sea again. My store is getting low here. But what do you intend to do, Jack?'

'Truth, Williams, I scarce know. I will make one trip to the farm, and if Mary is not as kind as I hope to find her I will be off too.'

Soon after breakfast I set off for the farmer's with an anxious heart. On my arrival I met Mary in the

yard. She seemed fluttered at sight of me but, sum-
moning up courage as I approached, she made a
distant bow and coldly asked me how I did. I now saw
there was no hope and had not recovered myself when
her father came out, and in a rough manner demanded
what I wanted and who I was. This in a moment
brought me to myself and, raising my head, which had
been bent towards the ground, I looked at him.

Mary shrunk from my gaze but the old man came
close up to me, and again demanded what I wanted.

'It is of no consequence,' I answered. Then,
looking at Mary, 'I believe I am an unwelcome
visitor—it is what I did not expect—so I will not
obtrude myself upon you any longer.' I then walked
off as indifferent to appearance as I could make
myself, but was tempted to look over my shoulder
more than once. I saw Mary in tears and her father
in earnest conversation with her.

I made up my mind to remain at the inn the rest
of that day and all night, in hopes of receiving an
appointment to meet Mary. I was loath to think I was
indifferent to her—and the feeling of being slighted
is so bitter I could have quarrelled with myself and all
the world. I sat with Williams at the window all day.
No message came. In the morning we bade adieu to
the fair jilts with heavy hearts—Williams for his
mother's and I for London.

After working a few weeks in London at my own
business, my wandering propensities came as strong
upon me as ever, and I resolved to embrace the first

opportunity to gratify it, no matter whither, only let me wander. I had been many times on the different wharfs looking for a vessel, but the seamen were so plenty there was great difficulty in getting a berth.

I met by accident Captain Bond, who hailed me and inquired if I wished a berth. He had been captain of a transport in the American war. I had favoured him at St John's. I answered him, 'It was what I was looking after.'

'Then, if you will, come and be cooper of the *Leviathan* Greenland ship. I am captain. You may go to Squire Mellish and say I recommend you for cooper.'

I thanked him for his goodwill, went, and was engaged and on board at work next day.

We sailed in a short time for the coast of Greenland, and touched at Lerwick, where we took on board what men we wanted. In the first of the season we were very unsuccessful, having very stormy weather. I at one time thought our doom was fixed. It blew a dreadful gale and we were for ten days completely fast in the ice. As far as we could see all was ice, and the ship was so pressed by it everyone thought we must either be crushed to pieces or forced out upon the top of the ice, there ever to remain.

At length the wind changed and the weather moderated, and where nothing could be seen but ice, in a short time after, all as far as the eye could reach was open sea. What were our feelings at this change it were vain to attempt a description of—it was a reprieve from death.

The horrors of our situation were far worse than any storm I ever was in. In a storm upon a lea-shore, there, even in all its horrors, there is exertion to keep the mind up, and a hope to weather it. Locked up in ice, all exertion is useless. The power you have to contend with is far too tremendous and unyielding. It, like a powerful magician, binds you in its icy circle, and there you must behold, in all its horrors, your approaching fate, without the power of exertion, while the crashing of the ice and the less loud but more alarming cracking of the vessel serve all to increase the horrors of this dreadful sea-mare.

When the weather moderated we were very successful and filled our ship with four fish.* I did not like the whale-fishing. There is no sight for the eye of the inquisitive after the first glance and no variety to charm the mind. Desolation reigns around: nothing but snow, or bare rocks and ice. The cold is so intense and the weather often so thick. I felt so cheerless that I resolved to bid adieu to the coast of Greenland for ever, and seek to gratify my curiosity in more genial climes.

We arrived safe in the river and proceeded up to our situation. But how strange are the freaks of fate! In the very port of London, as we were hurrying to our station, the tide was ebbing fast when the ship missed stays and yawed round, came right upon the Isle of Dogs, broke her back and filled with water.

* These were bowhead whales.

There was none of us hurt and we lost nothing as she was insured. I was one of those placed upon her to estimate the loss sustained amongst the casks, and was kept constantly on board for a long time.

5

Voyage to Grenada—Treatment of the Negroes—Dancing and Songs—Long-Shorers Chiefly Scots and Irishmen—Anecdote of a Welshman.

M Y NEXT VOYAGE was on board the *Cotton Planter* commanded by Captain Young, bound for the island of Grenada. I was very happy under Captain Young. He had been long in the Mediterranean trade where he had lost his health, and every year made a voyage to the West Indies to avoid the English winters. We sailed in the month of October, and arrived safe at St George's, Grenada.

I wrought a great deal on shore and had a number of blacks under me. They are a thoughtless, merry race; in vain their cruel situation and sufferings act upon their buoyant minds. They have snatches of joy that their pale and sickly oppressors never know. It may appear strange, yet it is only in the West Indian islands that the pictures of Arcadia are in a faint manner realised once in the week.

When their cruel situation allows their natural propensities to unfold themselves on the evenings of Saturday and Sabbath, no sound of woe is to be heard in this land of oppression—the sound of the Benji[†] and rattle, intermixed with song, alone is heard. I have seen them dancing and singing of an evening, and their backs sore from the lash of their cruel task-masters. I have lain upon deck of an evening, faint and exhausted from the heat of the day, to enjoy the

---

† The Benji is made of an old firkin [a small cask] with one end out, covered with shark skin, and beat upon with two pieces of wood. The rattles are made of a calabash shell, and a few small pebbles in it, fixed on a wooden handle; these they shake to the time of the Benji.

cool breeze of evening, and their wild music and song, the shout of mirth and dancing, resounded along the beach and from the valleys. There the negroes bounded in all the spirit of health and happiness while their oppressors could hardly drag their effeminate bodies along, from dissipation or the enervating effects of the climate.

These meetings are made up and agreed upon often long before they arrive. The poor and despised slaves will club their scanty earning for the refreshments and to pay Benji men. Many of them will come miles to be present. The females dress in all their finery for the occasion, and the males are decked with any fragments of dress they can obtain. Many of them are powdered. They all ape the manners of their masters as much as is in their power.

It is amusing to see them meet each other; they have so many congées, set phrases and kind inquiries in which Mama is the person most kindly inquired after.* They are as formal as dancing-masters, and make up to each other in civilities for the contempt heaped upon them by the whites.

The food allowed them by their masters is very poor. Half a salt herring, split down the middle, to each (they call it the one-eyed fish upon this account), horse beans and Indian corn constitute their fare. The Indian corn they must grind for themselves on Saturday after their day's task is done, which in general

---

* Congées: ways of saying hello and goodbye.

is to bring one burden of wood to the estate.

From Saturday until Monday morning they have to rest themselves and cultivate their patch of garden ground. Those who live near seaports prefer going to the mountains and gathering coconuts, plantains and other fruit which they sell. The slaves all bring any little fruit or vegetables they have to spare to market.

The sales by the whites, as well as blacks, are all made on the Sabbath day. The jailor of St George's is vendue-master by right of office, and none dare lift a hammer to sell without his permission.*

Captain Young did not keep his crew upon allowance. We had 'cut and come again' always. I often took a piece of lean beef and a few biscuits with me when I went to the plantation, as a present to the blacks. This the poor creatures would divide among themselves to a single fibre. As I had always been kind to them, they invited me and a few other seamen to one of their entertainments. I went with pleasure, to observe their ways more minutely. Upon my arrival I could hardly keep my gravity at their appearance, yet I esteemed them in my heart.

There was one black who acted as master of the ceremonies, but the Benji man appeared greater than any other individual. They all, before they commenced to dance, made their obeisance to him; the same at the conclusion. The master of ceremonies had an old cocked hat, and no courtier could have

* Vendue-master: auctioneer.

used it with more zeal. Many of the females had cast^r silk gowns which had belonged to their mistresses, and their heads powdered—but they were tawdry figures, though no lady or gentleman could have been more vain of their appearance or put on more airs.

The kind creatures had, upon our account, subscribed for three-bit maubi.† When they dance they accompany the Benji with the voice. Their songs were many of them *extempore*, and made on our ship or ourselves. My small gifts were not forgot. Their choruses are common. Their songs are of the simplest kind, as:

> I lost my shoe in an old canoe,
>> Johnio! come Winum so.
> I lost my boot in a pilot boat,
>> Johnio! come Winum so.

Others are satirical, as:

> My Massa a bad man,
>> My Missis cry honey,
> Is this the damn nigger,
>> You buy wi my money.
>> Ting a ring ting, ting a ring ting, tarro.

† Maubi is a drink like ginger-beer they drink among themselves, but as they knew sailors liked stouter drink, they bought rum. The price was one shilling and sixpence the gallon. A bit is equal to sixpence. Rum they call three-bit maubi.

Missis cry nigger man
   Do no work, but eattee;
She boil three eggs in pan,
   And gi the broth to me.
   Ting a ring ting, ting a ring ting, tarro.

With such songs as these they accompany the Benji. I do not recollect to have ever heard them sing a plaintive song, bewailing their cruel fate. This made me wonder much, as I expected they would have had many bewailing their destiny. But joy seems on these occasions their only aim.

The dance went on with spirit. I would have joined with pleasure, but it was beyond my strength after my day's work and the heat of the climate. We parted in good time without the least appearance of intoxication. I never in my life was happier, had more attention paid to me, or was more satisfied with an entertainment.

They have one rhyme they use at work, and adjust their motions to it. They never vary it that I heard.

Work away, body, bo
Work aa, jollaa.

In this manner they beguile the irksomeness of labour, but the capricious driver often interrupts their innocent harmony with the crack of his cart whip. No stranger can witness the cruelty unmoved.

George Innes and I were proceeding through the plantation to inform the master the double moses was

on the beach for sugar.† A black driver was flogging a woman big with child. Her cries rent the air, the other slaves declaring by their looks that sympathy they dared not utter. George ran to him and gave him a good beating, and swore he would double the gift if he laid another lash upon her. He had not dared when we returned.

There were two or three slaves upon the estate who, having once run away, had iron collars round their necks with long hooks that projected from them to catch the bushes should they run away again. These they wore night and day. There was a black slave, a cooper with a wooden leg, who had run away more than once. He was now chained to the block at which he wrought.

They are much given to talking and story-telling; the Scripture characters of the Old Testament are quite familiar to them. They talk with astonishment of Samson, Goliath, David, etc. I have seen them hold up their hands in astonishment at the strength of the white Buccaras. I have laughed at their personifications. Hurricane, they cannot conceive what it is. There are planters of the name of Kane on the island. Hurricane, they will say, 'He a strong white Buccara, he come from London.'

There was a black upon the estate who had been on the island of St Kitt's when Rodney defeated the

† The double moses is a large boat for taking on board the sugar casks. There are two, the single and double moses. The single holds only one hogshead, the double more.

French fleet. He had seen the action and was never tired speaking of it, nor his auditors of listening. He always concluded with this remark: 'The French 'tand 'tiff, but the English 'tand far 'tiffer. De all de same as game cock, de die on de 'pot.'

They are apt to steal, but are so very credulous they are easily detected. Captain Young gave a black butcher of the name of Coffee a hog to kill. When the captain went to see it, Coffee said, 'This very fine hog, Massa, but I never see a hog like him in all my life, he have no liver, no light.'*

Captain Young: 'That is strange, Coffee. Let me see in the book.' He took a memorandum book out of his pocket, turned over a few leaves, and looked very earnest. 'I see Coffee go to hell bottom—hog have liver and lights.'

Coffee shook like an aspen leaf, and said, 'O Massa, Coffee no go to hell bottom—hog have liver and lights.'

He restored them and, trembling, awaited his punishment. Captain Young only laughed, and made him a present of them.

I one time went with Captain Young to a planter's, where he was to dine, that I might accompany him back to the ship in the evening, as he was weakly. Upon our arrival I was handed over to a black who was butler and house steward. He had been in England and, as he said, seen London and King

* Light: lung.

George. He was by this become a greater man than by his situation among the other slaves, and was as vain in showing the little he knew as if he had been bred at college, and was perpetually astonishing the other slaves, whom he looked down upon, with the depth of his knowledge and his accounts of London and King George.

No professor could have delivered his opinions and observations with more pomp and dogmatism. One of the blacks inquired at me what kind of people the Welsh were. To enjoy the sport, as one of the crew, William Jones, a Welshman, was in company with me at the time, I referred him to the black oracle who, after considering a moment or two, replied with a smile of satisfaction upon his sooty features, 'The English have ships, the Irish have ships and the Scotch have ships, but Welshmen have no ships—they are like the negro man, they live in the bush.'

The Welshman started to his feet and would have knocked him down had I not prevented. He poured out a volley of oaths upon him.

He heard him with indifference, and his assertion was not the least shaken in the opinion of his hearers by the Welshman's violence—it, like many others of equal truth, was quoted and received as gospel. It was long a byword in the ship: 'Welshman live in the bush like negro man.'

Our cook having left the vessel, we were forced to take a long-shorer in his place. They are a set of idle dissipated seamen who will not work or take a berth.

They loiter along the harbours and get drunk by any means, no matter however base. Home they have none. The weather is so warm, they lie out all night and are content with little victuals. They are in general covered with rags and filth, the victims of idleness and disease. It is nothing uncommon to see their feet and ankles a mass of sores, their feet eaten by the jiggers until they resemble fowls' feet, having no flesh on them. Their minds chilled and totally sunk, death soon closes their career.

The next morning after the new cook came on board, he lay so long the captain's kettle was not boiled, nor the fire kindled. Paddy was quite indifferent when the cabin boy told him Captain Young must have the kettle immediately. He replied, 'Let him send his blasters and blowers here then.' Blasters and blowers was sent about his business immediately, and he cared not a fig.

I must confess the long-shorers are mostly composed of Irish and Scots. The very blacks despise them. They could make a good living by carrying water, as they could get a bit a burden. Many blacks get leave from the overseers to do this, giving them a bit a day, and earn as much as buy their freedom. An overseer may often have a dozen blacks thus employed, and his master not a bit the wiser, and the money his own gain.

We brought to England, as passenger from the island, a planter who was very rich and had a number of slaves. He had been a common seaman on board

of a man-of-war, had deserted and lived on shore concealed until his ship sailed. He afterwards married a free black woman who kept a punch-house, who died and left him above three thousand pounds. With this he had bought a plantation and slaves, and was making money fast. He brought as much fresh provisions and preserves on board as would have served ten men out and out, and was very kind to the men in giving them liquor and fresh provisions.

6

Voyage of Discovery—Anecdote—
Falkland Islands—Cape Horn—
Owhyee—Atooi—Onehow—Manners
of the Natives.

UPON OUR ARRIVAL in London I learned that my old officer, Lieutenant Portlock, now captain, was going out in the *King George*, as commander, in company with the *Queen Charlotte*, Captain Dixon, upon a voyage of discovery and trade round the world.

This was the very cruise I had long wished for. At once I made myself clean and waited upon Captain Portlock. He was happy to see me, as I was an excellent brewer of spruce-beer, and the very man he wished, but knew not where to have sent for me. I was at once engaged on the most liberal terms as cooper, and went away rejoicing in my good fortune. We had a charter from the South Sea Company and one from the India House, as it was to be a trading voyage for furs as well as discovery. This was in the year 1785. AET 30grs

With a joyful heart I entered on this voyage but, through an unforeseen accident, I had more to do than I engaged for. Our steward went on shore for a few necessary articles just before we sailed. He was a foolish lad, got tipsy, and the money sold him. Having spent it, he was ashamed to come on board again. The wind was fair, and I engaged to fill his place rather than delay the voyage one day, so eager was I upon it.

The first land we made was Santa Cruz in the island of Tenerife, where we stayed ten days getting fruit and provisions; then made the island of Sao Tiago (it belongs to the Portuguese) where we

watered and took in fresh provisions. While here we caught a number of fish called bass, very like salmon, which we eat fresh. The island is badly cultivated but abounds in cattle. We exchanged old clothes for sheep, or anything the men wanted.

The Portuguese here are great rogues. I bought two fat sheep from one of them. The bargain was made and I was going to lead away my purchase when he gave a whistle and my sheep scampered off to the fields. The fellow laughed at my surprise. I had a great mind to give him a beating for his trick, and take my clothes from him, but we had strict orders not to quarrel with the people upon any account. At length he made a sign that I might have them again by giving a few more articles. I had no alternative but lose what I had given or submit to his roguery. I gave a sign I would. He gave another whistle and the sheep returned to his side. I secured them before I gave the second price.

With all their roguery they are very careless of their money, more so than any people I ever saw. In walking through the town I have seen kegs full of dollars, without heads, standing in the houses, and the door open without a person in the house to look after them.

Having watered, we run for the Falkland Islands. When we arrived we found two American vessels busy whaling. We hoisted our colours, the Anchor and Hope. The Americans took us for Spaniards and set off in all haste. When we landed we found a great

number of geese ready plucked and a large fire burning, so we set to work and roasted as many as served us all, and enjoyed them much.

Next morning the Americans came near in their boats, and found out their mistake. Captain Portlock thanked them for their treat. We then had a busy time killing geese. There are two kinds, the water and upland. The water ones are very pretty, spreckled like a partridge. The penguins were so plenty we were forced to knock them out of our way as we walked along the beach.

The pelicans are plenty and build their nests of clay. They are near each other, like a honey-comb. I was astonished how each bird knew its own nest. They appear to hatch in the same nest until they are forced to change by the accumulation of dung. They are so tame I have stood close by when they arrived with their pouch distended with fish, and fed their young without being in the least disturbed.

We killed a number of hogs. Our doctor broke his double-barrelled gun in dispatching one, and sold it afterwards in China for £42. What was of more value to us was a great many iron hoops and beeswax, the remains of some wreck. We picked up some of the wax but took every inch of the hoops. They were more valuable than gold to us for trading with the natives.

When off Cape Horn we perceived an object floating at a small distance from the ship. Not one of us could make out what it was. All our boats being fast,

two men went down into the water and swam to it,
and made it fast in the slings. When it came on board
it was a cask, but so overgrown with weeds and bar-
nacles the bung-hole could not be discovered. I was
set to work to cut into it. To our agreeable surprise
it was full of excellent port wine. All the crew got a
little of it and Captain Portlock gave us brandy in
place of the rest.

We next made Staten Island; the weather was fine,
but very cold.* We stood away for latitude 23° where we
cruised about for some time in quest of islands laid down
in our charts. We could find none, but turtle in great
abundance. They were a welcome supply, but we soon
tired of them, cook them as we could in every variety.

Not finding the islands, we bore away for the
Sandwich Islands.** The first land we made was
Owhyee, the island where Captain Cook was killed.
The *King George* and *Queen Charlotte* were the first
ships which had touched there since that melancholy
event. The natives came on board in crowds and were
happy to see us. They recognised Portlock and others
who had been on the island before, along with Cook.
Our decks were soon crowded with hogs, breadfruit,
yams and potatoes. Our deck soon resembled sham-
bles—our butcher had fourteen assistants.

I was as busy and fatigued as I could be cutting iron
hoops into lengths of eight and nine inches which the

---

* Staten Island lies south of Tierra del Fuego.
** The Hawaiian Islands.

carpenter ground sharp. These were our most valuable commodity in the eyes of the natives. I was stationed down in the hold of the vessel, and the ladders were removed to prevent the natives from coming down to the treasury. The King of Owhyee looked to my occupation with a wistful eye; he thought me the happiest man on board to be among such vast heaps of treasure.

Captain Portlock called to me to place the ladder and allow the king to come down, and give him a good long piece. When the king descended he held up his hands and looked astonishment personified. When I gave him the piece of hoop of twenty inches long he retired a little from below the hatch into the shade, undid his girdle, bent the iron to his body and, adjusting his belt in the greatest haste, concealed it. I suppose he thought I had stole it. I could not but laugh to see the king concealing what he took to be stolen goods.*

We were much in want of oil for our lamps. The sharks abounding, we baited a hook with a piece of salt pork and caught the largest I ever saw in any sea. It was a female, nineteen feet long. It took all hands to hoist her on board; her weight made the vessel heel. When she was cut up we took forty-eight young ones out of her belly, eighteen inches long. We saw them go into her mouth after she was hooked.** The hook

---

* The king was more likely hiding it from his fellow Hawaiians.
** The fish seen apparently entering the mouth were probably not young sharks but remora (suckerfish) which habitually accompany larger marine organisms.

was fixed to a chain attached to our mainbrace, or we never would have kept her. It was evening when she snapped the bait; we hauled the head just above the surface, the swell washing over it. We let her remain thus all night and she was quite dead in the morning. There were in her stomach four hogs, four full-grown turtle, beside the young ones. Her liver, the only part we wanted, filled a tierce.*

Almost every man on board took a native woman for a wife while the vessel remained, the men thinking it an honour, or for their gain, as they got many presents of iron, beads or buttons. The women came on board at night and went on shore in the morning. In the evening they would call for their husbands by name. They often brought their friends to see their husbands, who were well pleased, as they were never allowed to go away empty.

The fattest woman I ever saw in my life our gunner chose for a wife. We were forced to hoist her on board. Her thighs were as thick as my waist. No hammock in the ship would hold her. Many jokes were cracked upon the pair.

They are the worst people to pronounce the English of any I ever was among. Captain Portlock they called *Potipoti*. The nearest approach they could make to my name was *Nittie*, yet they would make the greatest efforts, and look so angry at themselves and vexed at their vain efforts.

* A large cask of varying size.

We had a merry facetious fellow on board called Dickson. He sung pretty well. He squinted and the natives mimicked him. Abenoue, King of Atooi, could cock his eye like Dickson better than any of his subjects.* Abenoue called him Billicany, from his often singing 'Rule Britannia'. Abenoue learned the air and the words as near as he could pronounce them. It was an amusing thing to hear the king and Dickson sing. Abenoue loved him better than any man in the ship, and always embraced him every time they met on shore or in the ship, and began to sing, 'Tule Billicany, Billicany tule,' etc.

We had the chief on board who killed Captain Cook for more than three weeks. He was in bad health, and had a smelling-bottle with a few drops in it which he used to smell at. We filled it for him. There were a good many bayonets in possession of the natives, which they had obtained at the murder of Cook.

We left Owhyee and stood down to Atooi, where we watered and had a feast from Abenoue the King. We took our allowance of brandy on shore and spent a most delightful afternoon, the natives doing all in their power to amuse us. The girls danced, the men made a sham fight, throwing their spears. The women, standing behind, handed the spears to the men the same as in battle, thus keeping up a continued shower of spears. No words can convey an adequate

* Atooi: Kauai.

idea of their dexterity and agility. They thought we were bad with the rheumatism, our movements were so slow compared with their own. The women would sometimes lay us down and chafe and rub us, making moan and saying, 'O Rume! O Rume!' They wrestled, but the stoutest man in our ship could not stand a single throw with the least chance of success.

We next stood for Onehow, of which Abenoue was king as well as Atooi, to get yams.* This island grows them in abundance, and scarce any thing else. They have no wood upon the island but exchange their yams for it to build their canoes. While lying here it came to blow a dreadful gale. We were forced to cut our cables and stand out to sea, and leave sixteen men and boys. It was three weeks before we could return. When we arrived we found them well and hearty. These kind people had lodged them two and two in their houses, gave them plenty of victuals and liberty to ramble over the whole island.

The only man who was in the least alarmed for his safety was an old boatswain. He was in continual fear. The innocent natives could not meet to divert themselves, or even a few talk together, but the old sinner would shake with horror and called to his shipmates, 'Now, they are going to murder us—this is our last night.' He was a perfect annoyance to the others. He scarce ever left the beach but to go to some height to look out for the ships, and after looking till he was

* Onehow: Niihau.

almost blind he would seek out the other men to make his lamentations and annoy them with his fears of the loss of the ships or their being deserted by them.

At length we returned and took them on board, making presents to the king and his kind people for their unlimited hospitality. We now took an affectionate leave of these kind islanders.

As the summer now advanced apace we stood over to Cook's River, where we arrived in 1786, eleven months after we left England.* Upon our arrival a number of Russians came on board of us and made the captain a present of salmon, who in return gave them salt, an article they stood much in need of. One of our men, who spoke the Russian tongue, told them we were upon a voyage of discovery. We did not wish them to know we were trading in furs. We parted from them with mutual civilities.

At the entrance of Cook's River is an immense volcanic mountain which was in action at the time, and continued burning all the time we lay there, pouring down its side a torrent of lava as broad as the Thames. At night the sight was grand but fearful. The natives here had their spears headed with copper but, having no one on board who could speak their language, we had no means of learning where they obtained the copper.

While we lay here it was the heat of summer, yet the ice never melted and the snow was lying very deep

* Cook's River: Cook Inlet, Alaska.

on the heights. What a contrast from the delightful islands we had so lately left.

Our longboat, decked and schooner-rigged, proceeded up the river in hopes of finding an outlet, or inland sea. After proceeding with great difficulty and perseverance, until all hopes of success vanished, they returned. We then bore to the southward to Prince William's Sound to pursue our trade with the Indians. They are quite different from the Sandwich Islanders in appearance and habits. They are not cruel but great thieves.

I was employed on shore brewing spruce all day and slept on board at night. One night the Indians, after starting the beer, carried off all the casks: they were iron-hooped.* All our search was vain; no traces of them were to be discovered. To quarrel with the Indians would have defeated the object of our voyage. At length they were discovered by accident in the most unlikely place, in the following manner.

One of our boats had been on a trading excursion detained so long, we became alarmed for its safety. Captain Portlock sent some of our men armed to the top of a high hill to look out for the boat. To the surprise of the men, they found the staves and ends of the barrels, and some large stones they had used in breaking them to pieces. How great must their labour have been in rolling up the barrels and then in dashing them to pieces. Yet I have no doubt

* Starting: spilling.

they thought themselves richly rewarded in obtaining the iron hoops. The men brought back a stave or two with the ship's name branded on them to evidence the truth of their discovery. We then moved the brewing place to the other side of the island, within sight of the ship.

I was much annoyed by the natives for some time while working. They would handle the hoops, and every now and then a piece would vanish. There was only a quarter-master and boy with me. While the natives swarmed around I felt rather uncomfortable. They became more and more bold. The captain, seeing from the deck my disagreeable situation, hailed me to set Neptune, our great Newfoundland dog, upon them, saying he would fear them more than fifty men.

I obeyed with alacrity and hounded Neptune, who enjoyed the sport as much as I, to see the great fellows run, screaming like girls, in all directions. I was soon left to pursue my labour unmolested and whenever they grew troublesome Neptune, without orders, put them to the running and screaming. When one approached, if Neptune was near, he would stretch out his arms, and cry, '*Lally, Neptune*'—that is 'friend' in their language. The Indians here could pronounce every word we spoke almost as well as ourselves. This appeared the more strange after hearing the vain efforts of our friends the Sandwich Islanders.

One Sabbath day all the ship's company, except the captain, two boys and the cook, were on shore

amusing themselves. During our absence an immense number of the natives came alongside and took complete possession of the vessel and helped themselves to whatever took their fancy. The captain, boys, and cook barricadoed themselves in the cabin and loaded all the muskets and pistols within their reach. Their situation was one of great danger.

The surgeon and myself were the first that arrived on the beach. The captain hailed us from the cabin window and let us know his disagreeable situation, telling us to force the Indians to put us on board. We having our muskets, they complied at once. Thus, by adding strength to the captain, we gained new assurance and, the others doing as we did, were put all on board as they came to the beach. The Indians offered no violence to the ship and when the crew were nearly all on board they began to leave the vessel, shipping off their booty.

Captain Portlock ordered us to take no notice of the transaction in way of hurting the Indians but to purchase back the articles they had taken away that were of use to us —but they had only taken what pieces of iron they found loose about the ship. After having hid the things they had stolen they began to trade as if nothing had happened, and we bought back what few bolts they had taken.

They had plundered the smith's tent in the same manner, although they looked upon him as a greater man than the captain. He was a smart young fellow and kept the Indians in great awe and wonder. They

thought the coals were made into powder.* I have seen them steal small pieces and bruise them, then come back. When he saw this, he would spit upon the anvil while working the hot iron and give a blow upon it. They would run away in fear and astonishment when they heard the crack.

* Powder: gun powder.

7

Trading Voyages—Conduct of the Natives—Sandwich Islands— Language—Nootka Sound—Ships Sail for China.

ONE OR OTHER of our boats, often both, were absent for some time upon trading voyages. In one of these trips our boat was nearly cut off, and would in all probability, had it not been for the presence of mind of an American, one of the crew, Joseph Laurence. I never was more alarmed for my safety in the whole voyage.

We were rowing through a lagoon to get a near cut to the ship. The tide was ebbing fast, the boat took the ground, and before we could do anything to get her off the whole bay was dry. The natives surrounded the boat in great numbers and looked very mischievous. We knew not what to do.

In this dilemma, Laurence, who knew their ways, took a small keg of molasses and went to the beach. At the same time he sat down by it and began to sing and lick, inviting them to follow his example. They licked and listened to him for a good while, and even joined him in singing—but the molasses wore done and they were weary of his songs.

We looked about in great anxiety and discovered a small height that commanded the boat. To this we ran but dared not to fire, even while they were plundering the boat. They could have killed us all with spears and stones, had we even shot one hundred of them and wasted all our ammunition.

We stood like bears at the stake, expecting them every moment to commence the attack, resolved to sell our lives as dear we could. At length the wished return of tide came and we got to the boat, and she

floated soon after. Then we cared not one penny for them. We began to trade and bought back the articles they had stolen. Even our compass we were forced to buy back. We set sail for the *King George*, resolved to be more circumspect in future and happy we had escaped so well.

The party who had taken possession of the vessel on the Sabbath day, the next time they came back had their faces blacked and their heads powdered with the down of birds. They had done this as a disguise, which showed they had a consciousness of right and wrong. Thinking we knew them not, as we took no notice of them, they were as merry and funny as any of the rest.

While the boats were absent on a trading voyage the canoe was sent to haul the seine for salmon. There were fourteen men and boys in it. About half way between the vessel and the shore she filled with water. Those who could swim made for the beach. The boys, and those who could not, clung to the canoe. Captain Portlock saw from the deck the danger they were in and requested the boatswain, who was an excellent swimmer, to go to their assistance. He refused.

The sailmaker and myself leapt into the water. I had a line fixed round my waist, as I swam first, which he supported at a short distance behind, to ease its weight. When I came up to the canoe they were nearly spent. I fixed the line to the canoe and we made a signal to the ship when those on board drew her to the vessel, John Butler and I attending to assist and encourage them. There was a son of Sir John Dick's

and a son of Captain Gore's among the boys. Captain Portlock never could bear the boatswain afterwards. Before this he was a great favourite.

While in Prince William's Sound the boat went on an excursion to Snug Corner Cove at the top of the Sound. She discovered the *Nootka*, Captain Mairs, in a most distressing situation from the scurvy. There were only the captain and two men free from disease. Two and twenty Lascars had died through the course of the winter. They had caused their own distress by their inordinate use of spirits on Christmas eve. They could not bury their own dead. They were only dragged a short distance from the ship and left upon the ice. They had muskets fixed upon the capstan and man-ropes that went down to the cabin, that when any of the natives attempted to come on board they might fire them off to scare them.

They had a large Newfoundland dog whose name was Towser, who alone kept the ship clear of the Indians. He lay day and night upon the ice before the cabin window, and would not allow the Indians to go into the ship. When the natives came to barter they would cry, '*Lally Towser*,' and make him a present of a skin before they began to trade with Captain Mairs, who lowered from the window his barter, and in the same way received their furs.

The *Beaver*, the *Nootka's* consort, had been cut off in the beginning of the winter and none of her people were ever heard of. We gave him every assistance in our power in spruce and molasses, and two of our

crew to assist in working the vessel, Dickson and George Willis, who stopped at Canton until we arrived then, wishing him well, took our leave of him. Captain Portlock could have made a fair prize of him, as he had no charter and was trading in our limits, but he was satisfied with his bond not to trade on our coast; but the bond was forfeit as soon as we sailed, and he was in China before us.

We now stood for Nootka Sound, but encountered a dreadful gale and were blown off the coast and suffered much in our sails and rigging which caused us to stand for the Sandwich Islands to refit—which gave us great joy.

The American coast is a hostile region compared with the Sandwich Islands. The American Indians are very jealous, and if any of our men were found with their women, using the least freedom, they would take his life if it was in their power; but their women are far from being objects of desire, they are so much disfigured by slitting their lips and placing large pieces of wood in them shaped like a saucer. I have seen them place berries upon it, and shake them into their mouth as a horse would corn out of a mouth-bag, or lick them in with their tongue. The men have a bone eight inches long, polished and stuck through the gristle of their nose. We called it their sprit-sailyard. We had suffered a good deal of hardship on this coast, and bade it adieu with joy.

Soon as we arrived at Owhyee our old acquaintance flocked on board to welcome us, each with a

present. Then such a touching of noses and shaking of hands took place. '*Honi, honi*'—that is, touch nose, and 'How are you?'—were the only words to be heard. Our deck was one continued scene of joy. I was now picking up the language pretty fast and could buy and sell in it, and knew a great number of words that were very useful to me. There is a great likeness in many of their words to the Latin:

Sandwich Islands	English
terra	earth
nuna	moon
sola	sun
oma	man
leo	dog

Noue is their word for large, *maccou* for a fish-hook. When they saw our anchors they held up their hands and said, '*Noue maccou.*' During our wintering this second time, almost the same scenes were re-acted.

Having refitted and taken in provisions, we again set sail for Cook's River, Prince William's and Nootka Sound to obtain more fur skins. We were pretty successful. While on shore in Prince William's Sound, brewing spruce beer, I and the quartermaster made an excursion up the river and discovered a large space covered with snake-root, which is of great value in China.* My comrade, who had been in China,

* This was probably ginseng (*Panax spp.*) which has a forked root.

informed me of its value. It is the sweetest smelling plant I ever was near when it is growing. We set to work and dug up as much as we chose and dried it, letting no one know, for lessening the value of what we got. It was got safe on board the day before we sailed and we sold it well at Wampoa.*

We parted company from the *Queen Charlotte*. She had been absent for a long time. When a party of Indians came to the *King George*, having in their possession a pair of buckles that belonged to one of the people on board our consort, we became alarmed for her, thinking she had been cut off. We immediately set sail for Nootka Sound, leaving a large quantity of salmon half dried. After waiting in Nootka Sound, our place of rendezvous, for some time, and she not appearing, we immediately set sail for Owhyee, but got no word of our consort until we came to Atooi, when we perceived Abenoue in his single canoe, making her scud through the water, crying, '*Tattoo for Potipoti*,' as he jumped upon deck with a letter from Captain Dixon, which removed our fears and informed us he had discovered an island and got a very great number of skins and had sailed for China. We watered and laid in our provisions as quick as we could to follow her.

Abenoue, soon after he came on board, told the captain he had seen Billicany, and squinted so like Dickson we knew at once Mairs had been there in the

* Wampoa: a port town just outside Canton.

Nootka. Dickson afterwards told us Mairs would not
have got anything from Abenoue had he and Willis
not been with him.

Abenoue had a son called Poinoue—in English
'Large Pudding'. I thought him well named. He had
the largest head of any boy I ever saw. His father
wished Captain Portlock to take him to England but
Poinoue did not wish to go. He leapt overboard just
as we sailed and swam back to his father.

It was with a sensation of regret I bade a final adieu
to the Sandwich Islands. Even now I would prefer
them to any country I ever was in. The people so kind
and obliging, the climate so fine and provisions so
abundant—all render it a most endearing place.

Owhyee is the only place I was not ashore in.
Captain Portlock never went himself and would not
allow his crew to go. The murder of Cook made him
timorous of trusting too much to the islanders. At
Atooi and Onehow we went on shore, one watch one
day, the other the next.

After taking on board as much provisions as we
could stow we sailed for China. At the Ladrones, or
Mariana Islands, a number of pilots came on board.
The captain agreed with one. The bargain was made
in the following manner. He showed the captain the
number of dollars he wished by the number of cass, a
small brass coin, the captain taking from the number
what he thought too much, the pilot adding when he
thought it too little. He was to pilot the *King George*
to the island of Macau. From thence we sailed up the

Bocca Tigris to Wampoa, where we sold our cargo of skins.* We were engaged to take home a cargo of tea for the East India Company.

* Bocca Tigris: the estuary at the head of which Canton is situated.

8

China—Manners of the Chinese—
Food—Religion—Punishments—
Evasion of Duty—St Helena—
Author Arrives in England.

I WAS AS happy as any person ever was to see anything. I scarcely believed I was so fortunate as really to be in China. As we sailed up the river, I would cast my eyes from side to side. The thoughts and ideas I had pictured in my mind of it were not lessened in brilliancy, rather increased. The immense number of buildings that extended as far as the eye could reach, their fantastic shapes and gaudy colours, their trees and flowers so like their paintings, and the myriads of floating vessels, and above all the fanciful dresses and gaudy colours of their clothes—all serve to fix the mind of a stranger upon his first arrival. But upon a nearer acquaintance he is shocked at the quantity of individual misery that forces itself upon his notice, and gradually undoes the grand ideas he had formed of this strange people.

Soon as we cast anchor the vessel was surrounded with sampans. Every one had some request to make. Tartar girls requested our clothes to wash, barbers to shave the crews, others with fowls to sell; indeed, every necessary we could want. The first we made bargain with was a barber, Tommy Linn. He agreed to shave the crew for the six months we were to be there for half a dollar from each man, and he would shave every morning, if we chose, on board the ship, coming off in his sampan.

The Tartar girls washed our clothes for the broken meat or what rice we left at mess. They came every day in their sampans and took away the men's shirts, bringing them back the next, and never mixed the

clothes. They all spoke less or more English and would jaw with the crew as fast as any women of their rank in England. They had a cage-like box fixed to the stern of their sampan in which was a pig who fed and fattened there at his ease.

Our ears were dinned with the cry of the beggars in their sampans, '*Kamscha me lillo rice*'. I have seen the mandarins plunder these objects of compassion when they had been successful in their appeals to the feelings of the seamen. I was surprised at the minute subdivision of their money. Their cass is a small piece of base coin with a square hole in it, three of which are a kandarin; sixty cass one mace; one mace equal to sevenpence English money. The cass is of no use out of the country, and when a seaman changes a dollar he receives no other coin from the wily Chinese.

I was on shore for a good while at Wampoa, making candle for our voyage home. I had a number of Chinese under me. My greatest difficulty was to prevent them from stealing the wax. They are greater and more dexterous thieves than the Indians. A bambooing for theft, I really believe, confers no disgrace upon them.

They will allow no stranger to enter the city of Canton. I was different times at the gate, but all my ingenuity could not enable me to cross the bar, although I was eight days in the suburbs. The Tartars are not even allowed to sleep on shore. They live in junks and other craft upon the river. If employed on

shore they must be away by sunset, but may land again at sunrise in the morning.

The Chinese, I really believe, eat anything there is life in. Neptune was constantly on shore with me at the tent. Every night he caught less or more rats. He never eat them, but laid them down when dead at the tent door. In the morning the Chinese gave vegetables for them and were as well pleased as I was at the exchange.

After the candles were made I removed to Banks Hall to repair the cooper work, and screen sand and dry it, to pack the tea boxes for our voyage home. One day a boy was meddling rather freely with the articles belonging to me. Neptune bit him. I was extremely sorry for it, and after beating him dressed the boy's hurt which was not severe. I gave the boy a few cass, who went away quite pleased. In a short time after I saw him coming back, and his father leading him. I looked for squalls, but the father only asked a few hairs out from under Neptune's foreleg, close to the body. He would take them from no other part, and stuck them all over the wound.* He went away content. I had often heard, when a person had been tipsy the evening before, people tell him to take a hair of the dog that bit him, but never saw it in the literal sense before.

A short time before we sailed all the crew got two months' pay advance for private trade, and purchased

---

* Perhaps this was a folk preventative against rabies.

what articles they chose. The dollars are all stamped by the captain, as the Chinese are such cheats they will dexterously return you a bad dollar and assert, if not marked, it was the one you gave.

With all their roguery they are not ungrateful. One day two Chinese boys were playing in our boat. One of them fell overboard. The current was strong and the boy was carried down with rapidity. I leapt into the river and saved him with great difficulty, as the current bore us both along until my strength was almost spent. By an effort I got into the smooth water, and soon had the pleasure of delivering him to his father, who stood on the beach wringing his hands.

I wished to go on board, but the Chinese would have me to his house where I was most kindly received and got my dinner in great style. I like their manner of setting out the table at dinner. All that is to be eaten is placed upon the table at once, and all the liquors at the same time. You have all before you and you may make your choice. I dined in different houses and the same fashion was used in them all. The Chinese never thought he could show me kindness enough.

We buried our chief-mate, Mr Macleod, whose funeral I attended, upon French Island.

Almost every junk has a mandarin on board who keeps order and collects the revenue and tyrannises over the poor Chinese. They pay money for the liberty of doing anything to obtain a living. Tommy Linn paid seventy dollars for leave to practise as barber and surgeon upon the river.

They cure every disease by herbs. When any sailor or officer was so imprudent as visit Loblob Creek and received the reward of their folly, our surgeons could not cure them, yet the Chinese barber did so with ease.*

Every new moon all the men in China must have their heads shaved. If they do not the mandarin makes them suffer for it.

They have the longest nails to their fingers I ever saw. Many of their nails are half as long as the rest of the finger, they take so much care of them and keep them so white and clean. They, I really believe, would almost as soon have their throats cut as their nails. A Chinese will hold, by their means, more dollars in one hand than an Englishman will hold in both of his. Shaking hands will never be the fashion in China.

When the day is wet or thick, which rarely happens, the Chinese will say, 'Joss too much angry.' Then the paper sacrifices begin. The whole river is in a smoke. Every junk, down to the small sampan, must burn, under the direction of the mandarin, a certain quantity of paper to please 'Joss' their god. The rich must burn fine gilt paper, the poor coarser paper. The mandarin is the sole judge of the quantity and quality—from him there is no appeal. He himself burns no paper; a small piece of touchwood serves his turn. There he will stand in a conspicuous place, and look as steadfast upon it as a statue, until it is all burnt out.

* Loblob Creek: the local red-light district.

They are the most oppressed people I ever was amongst. They must want even a wife if they are not rich enough to pay the tax imposed by the mandarin. They are summary in their justice. Wherever the theft is committed, there the mandarin causes the culprit to be laid upon his back and beat upon the belly with a bamboo the number of times he thinks adequate to the offence. If the offence is great, they are sent to the Ladrone Islands, their place of banishment for thieves. There they live by piloting vessels and fishing but are not allowed to come up farther than Macau. They are cowardly and cruel. Six half-drunk sailors would clear a whole village; but when they catch one of them drunk and by himself, then they bamboo him in the cruellest manner.

Tommy Linn the barber was the agent we employed. He brought us any article we wanted from the city and, like his brethren in Europe, was a walking newspaper. His first word every morning was, 'Hey, yaw, what fashion?' and we used the same phrase to him. One morning he came, and the first thing he said was, 'Hey, yaw, what fashion? Soldier man's ship come to Lingcome bar.' We, after a few hours, heard that a man-of-war frigate had arrived at the mouth of the river. They are allowed to come no higher up. Tommy had seen the red coats of the marines.

They are much alarmed at the appearance of a man-of-war ship, and they often say, 'Englishman too much cruel, too much fight.' There were some

English seamen flogged for mutiny while we lay in the river. The Chinese wept like children for the men, saying, 'Hey, yaw, Englishman too much cruel, too much flog, too much flog.'

Having completed our cargo, we fell down the river. As we came near to the chop-house where the chop-marks are examined (the men having many articles on board in their private trade that had not paid duty, which the Chinese would have seized), we fell upon the old stratagem. When their boat put off two of us fell a fighting and we made the whole deck a scene of riot. These timorous Chinese custom-house-officers did not offer to come on board, but called out, 'Hey, yaw, what fashion? Too much baubry, too much baubry,' and put back to the chop-house.

By this manoeuvre we paid not one farthing of duty for our skins which we sold in China—the officers dared not come on board. We landed them as soon as possible and, when once in the factory, all was safe.

We set sail for St Helena where we made a present to the governor of a number of empty bottles. He in return gave us a present of potatoes, a valuable gift to us. While here, I and a number of the crew were nearly poisoned by eating albicores and bonettos.* We split and hung them in the rigging to dry. The moon's rays have the effect of making them

---

* Albicores and bonettos: fish similar to tuna and mackerel.

poisonous. My face turned red and swelled, but the others were far worse. Their heads were swelled twice their ordinary size—but we all recovered.

In a few days we set sail for England where I arrived without any remarkable occurrence after an absence of three years, having in that time circumnavigated the globe. We came into the river in the month of September 1788.

9

Author Engaged as Steward of a Convict Ship—Anecdotes of Female Convicts—Sails for New South Wales—Attaches Himself to Sarah Whitlam—Singular Punishment—Crossing the Line—Miscellaneous Occurrences—Port Jackson—St Helena.

I NOW RETURNED to Scotland with a sensation of joy only to be felt by those who have
been absent for some time. Every remembrance was
rendered more dear, every scene was increased in
beauty. A piece of oaten cake tasted far sweeter in my
mouth than the luxuries of eastern climes.

I was for a time reconciled to remain. The love of
country overcame my wandering habits. I had some
thought of settling for life, as I had saved a good deal
of my pay. In the middle of these musings, and before
I had made up my mind, a letter I received from
Captain Portlock upset all my future plans and rekin-
dled my wandering propensities with as great vigour
as ever.

The letter requested me to come to London
without delay, as there were two ships lying in the
river bound for New South Wales: the *Guardian* and
Lady Julian, in either of which I might have a berth.*
The *Guardian* was loaded with stores and necessaries
for the settlement. There was a vine-dresser and a
person to superintend the cultivation of hemp on
board. She sailed long before us. The *Lady Julian* was
to take out female convicts.

I would have chosen the *Guardian*, only she was a
man-of-war, and as I meant to settle in Scotland upon
our return I could not have left her when I chose. My
only object was to see the country, not to remain at
sea. I therefore chose the *Lady Julian*, as she was a

* This was the *Lady Juliana* which sailed with the second fleet.

transport, although I did not by any means like her cargo—yet to see the country I was resolved to submit to a great deal.

I was appointed steward of the *Lady Julian*, commanded by Captain Aitkin, who was an excellent humane man and did all in his power to make the convicts as comfortable as their circumstances would allow. The government agent, an old lieutenant, had been discharged a little before I arrived for cruelty to the convicts. He had even begun to flog them in the river. Government, the moment they learned the fact, appointed another in his place.

We lay six months in the river before we sailed, during which time all the jails in England were emptied to complete the cargo of the *Lady Julian*. When we sailed there were on board 245 female convicts.* There were not a great many very bad characters. The greater number were for petty crimes, and a great proportion for only being disorderly, that is, street-walkers, the colony at the time being in great want of women.

One, a Scottish girl, broke her heart and died in the river. She was buried at Dartford. Four were pardoned on account of his Majesty's recovery. The poor young Scottish girl I have never yet got out of my mind. She was young and beautiful, even in the convict dress, but pale as death, and her eyes red with weeping.

* The *Lady Juliana* actually carried 226 convicts.

She never spoke to any of the other women or came on deck. She was constantly seen sitting in the same corner from morning to night. Even the time of meals roused her not. My heart bled for her—she was a countrywoman in misfortune. I offered her consolation but her hopes and heart had sunk. When I spoke she heeded me not, or only answered with sighs and tears. If I spoke of Scotland she would wring her hands and sob until I thought her heart would burst. I endeavoured to get her sad story from her lips but she was silent as the grave to which she hastened. I lent her my Bible to comfort her but she read it not. She laid it on her lap after kissing it, and only bedewed it with her tears. At length she sunk into the grave of no disease but a broken heart. After her death we had only two Scottish women on board, one of them a Shetlander.

I went every day to the town to buy fresh provisions and other necessaries for them. As their friends were allowed to come on board to see them, they brought money; and numbers had it of their own, particularly a Mrs Barnsley, a noted sharper and shoplifter.* She herself told me her family for one

---

* Elizabeth Barnsley was fashionably dressed and 'had every appearance of gentility' when she visited an expensive draper's shop in Bond Street in February 1788, in the company of Ann Wheeler. They bought some muslin and Irish cloth, but a shop assistant noticed that Wheeler had slipped a whole bolt of muslin under her cloak and muff. Both women were convicted of theft, and Elizabeth spent over a year in

hundred years back had been swindlers and highway-men. She had a brother, a highwayman, who often came to see her as well dressed and genteel in his appearance as any gentleman. She petitioned the government agent and captain to be allowed to wear her own clothes in the river, and not the convict dress. This could on no account be allowed, but they told her she might wear what she chose when once they were at sea.

The agent, Lieutenant Edgar, had been with Captain Cook, was a kind humane man and very good to them. He had it in his power to throw all their clothes overboard when he gave them the convict dress, but he gave them to me to stow in the after hold, saying, 'They would be of use to the poor creatures when they arrived at Port Jackson.'

Those from the country came all on board in irons, and I was paid half a crown a head by the country jailors, in many cases, for striking them off upon my anvil, as they were not locked but riveted. There was a Mrs Davis, a noted swindler, who had obtained great quantities of goods under false names and other equally base means.*

* Two women with the surname of Davis were on board the *Lady Juliana*. The younger, Ann, was sentenced to seven

Newgate prison where she paid half a crown a week to stay in a relatively comfortable part of the prison. She joined her husband in Sydney where she bore him two sons. The family presumably returned to England after 1795. (See Michael Flynn, *The Second Fleet: Britain's Grim Convict Armada of 1790*, Library of Australian History, Sydney, 1993, 150.)

We had one Mary Williams, transported for receiving stolen goods.* She and other eight had been a long time in Newgate where Lord George Gordon had supported them. I went once a week to him and got their allowance from his own hand all the time we lay in the river.

One day I had the painful task to inform the father and mother of one of the convicts that their daughter, Sarah Dorset, was on board. They were decent-looking people, and had come to London to inquire after her. When I met them they were at Newgate. The jailor referred them to me. With tears in her eyes the mother implored me to tell her if such a one was on board. I told them there was one of that name. The father's heart seemed too full to allow him to speak but the mother with streaming eyes blessed God that they had found their poor lost child, undone as she was.

---

* Two convicts named Mary Williams sailed with Nicol. The one apparently referred to by Nicol had a tragic story to tell. Desperate to pay the rent of half a crown per week due on her room, she pawned a pair of sheets, two blankets and a pillow belonging to the room. She was sentenced to seven years' transportation but spent eighteen months in Newgate prison waiting for the sentence to be carried out. She was twenty-four when she embarked on the *Lady Juliana*. (See *The Second Fleet*, 613.)

---

years' transportation for trying to sell stolen clothing. The older, Deborah, had been sentenced to death (later commuted to transportation) for stealing jewellery from Mr Timothy Topping of Chislehurst. It is probably Deborah that Nicol is talking of here. (See *The Second Fleet*, 235-36.)

117

I called a coach, drove to the river and had them put on board. The father, with a trembling step, mounted the ship's side, but we were forced to lift the mother on board. I took them down to my berth and went for Sarah Dorset. When I brought her the father said in a choking voice, 'My lost child!' and turned his back, covering his face with his hands. The mother, sobbing, threw her hands around her. Poor Sarah fainted and fell at their feet. I knew not what to do. At length she recovered and in the most heart-rending accents implored their pardon.

She was young and pretty and had not been two years from her father's house at this present time, so short had been her course of folly and sin. She had not been protected by the villain that ruined her above six weeks, then she was forced by want upon the streets and taken up as a disorderly girl, then sent on board to be transported. This was her short but eventful history. One of our men, William Power, went out to the colony when her time was expired, brought her home and married her.*

I witnessed many moving scenes, and many of the most hardened indifference. Numbers of them would

---

* Sarah Dorset was convicted of stealing a greatcoat from a London pub. She was sentenced to seven years' transportation. Sarah in fact bore a son to Edward Powell, a seaman on the *Lady Juliana*. Powell did return to Sydney in 1793 but he then married Elizabeth Fish, a free woman, who returned with him to England. Sarah became housekeeper to John Woodward, butcher. The couple had three children. Sarah died in New South Wales in 1838. (See *The Second Fleet*, 248.)

not take their liberty as a boon. They were thankful for their present situation, so low had vice reduced them. Many of these from the country jails had been allowed to leave it to assist in getting in the harvest, and voluntarily returned.

When I inquired their reason, they answered, 'How much more preferable is our present situation to what it has been since we commenced our vicious habits? We have good victuals and a warm bed. We are not ill treated or at the mercy of every drunken ruffian as we were before. When we rose in the morning we knew not where we would lay our heads in the evening, or if we would break our fast in the course of the day. Banishment is a blessing for us. Have we not been banished for a long time, and yet in our native land, the most dreadful of all situations? We dared not go to our relations whom we had disgraced. Other people would shut their doors in our faces. We were as if a plague were upon us, hated and shunned.'

Others did all in their power to make their escape. These were such as had left their associates in rapine on shore and were hardened to every feeling but the abandoned enjoyments of their companions. Four of these made their escape on the evening before we left England through the assistance of their confederates on shore. They gave the man on watch gin to drink as he sat on the quarterdeck, the others singing and making fun. These four slipped over her bows into a boat provided for their escape. I never heard if they were retaken. We sailed without them.

Mrs Nelly Kerwin, a female of daring habits, banished for life for forging seamen's powers of attorney and personating their relations, when on our passage down the river, wrote to London for cash to some of her friends.* She got a letter informing her it was waiting for her at Dartmouth. We were in Colson Bay when she got this letter. With great address she persuaded the agent that there was an express for him and money belonging to her lying at Dartmouth. A man was sent who brought on board Nell's money, but no express for the agent. When she got it she laughed in his face and told him he was in her debt for a lesson. He was very angry, as the captain often told him Kerwin was too many for him.

We had on board a girl pretty well behaved, who was called by her acquaintance a daughter of Pitt's.**

---

* Eleanor Kirvein kept a 'house of entertainment for sailors' at Gosport. An important part of her business was 'bomb-boating'—providing credit and accommodation for sailors and finding them berths on outward-bound ships. She was convicted of forging the will of a seaman and was sentenced to death. After a 'panel of matrons' found her to be pregnant her sentence was commuted to transportation for seven years. She married Henry Palmer, a convict, in July 1790. A few months later he was killed by a falling tree. She sailed for India, a free woman, in 1793. Michael Flynn notes that she was probably one of the few convict mothers who lived to see the children they left behind. (See *The Second Fleet*, 386.)

** William Pitt (1759-1806) was the current prime minister of Great Britain.

She herself never contradicted it. She bore a most striking likeness to him in every feature and could scarce be known from him as to looks. We left her at Port Jackson.

Some of our convicts I have heard even to boast of the crimes and murders committed by them and their accomplices, but the far greater number were harmless unfortunate creatures, the victims of the basest seduction. With their histories, as told by themselves, I shall not trouble the reader.

When we were fairly out to sea, every man on board took a wife from among the convicts, they nothing loath. The girl with whom I lived, for I was as bad in this point as the others, was named Sarah Whitlam. She was a native of Lincoln, a girl of a modest reserved turn, as kind and true a creature as ever lived. I courted her for a week and upwards, and would have married her on the spot had there been a clergyman on board.

She had been banished for a mantle she had borrowed from an acquaintance. Her friend prosecuted her for stealing it, and she was transported for seven years.*

---

* Sarah Whitlam, who was born in 1767, was in fact convicted of the theft of a large amount of cloth and clothing, including six yards of black chintz cotton, a raven grey Coventry tammy gown, a pink quilted petticoat, a pair of stays, a fine white lawn apron, a chocolate ground silk handkerchief, a woman's black silk hat and a pair of leather shoes. Flynn speculates that her loot would have filled a cart and may have been stolen from a shop. (See *The Second Fleet*, 610.)

I had fixed my fancy upon her from the moment I knocked the rivet out of her irons upon my anvil, and as firmly resolved to bring her back to England when her time was out, my lawful wife, as ever I did intend anything in my life. She bore me a son in our voyage out.

What is become of her, whether she is dead or alive, I know not. That I do not is no fault of mine, as my narrative will show.

But to proceed. We soon found that we had a troublesome cargo, yet not dangerous or very mischievous—as I may say, more noise than danger. When any of them, such as Nance Ferrel who was ever making disturbance, became very troublesome we confined them down in the hold and put on the hatch.* This, we were soon convinced, had no effect as they became in turns outrageous, on purpose to be confined. Our agent and the captain wondered at the change in their behaviour.

I, as steward, found it out by accident. As I was overhauling the stores in the hold I came upon a hogshead of bottled porter with a hole in the side of it and, in place of full, there were nothing but empty bottles in it. Another was begun and more than a box of candles had been carried off. I immediately told the captain, who now found out the

---

* Elizabeth Farrell was convicted of stealing clothing and linen from a house in East Smithfield. She eventually went to Van Diemen's Land where she lived comfortably with her husband John Hall, a first-fleet convict. She died in Hobart in 1827. (See *The Second Fleet*, 268.)

cause of the late insubordination and desire of confinement.

We were forced to change the manner of punishing them. I was desired by the agent Lieutenant Edgar, who was an old lieutenant of Cook's, to take a flour barrel and cut a hole in the top for their head and one on each side for their arms. This we called a wooden jacket. Next morning, Nance Ferrel, as usual, came to the door of the cabin and began to abuse the agent and captain. They desired her to go away between decks and be quiet. She became worse in her abuse, wishing to be confined and sent to the hold, but to her mortification the jacket was produced, and two men brought her upon deck and put it on.

She laughed and capered about for a while, and made light of it. One of her comrades lighted a pipe and gave it her. She walked about strutting and smoking the tobacco, and making the others laugh at the droll figure she made. She walked a minuet, her head moving from side to side like a turtle.

The agent was resolved she should be heartily tired, and feel in all its force the disagreeableness of her present situation. She could only walk or stand— to sit or lie down was out of her power. She began to get weary and begged to be released. The agent would not until she asked his pardon, and promised amendment in future. This she did in humble terms before evening, but in a few days was as bad as ever. There was no taming her by gentle means. We were forced to tie her up like a man, and give her one dozen

with the cat-o'-nine-tails, and assure her of a clawing every offence. This alone reduced her to any kind of order.

How great was the contrast between her and Mary Rose. Mary was a timid modest girl who never joined in the ribaldry of the rest, neither did she take up with any man upon the voyage. She was a wealthy farmer's daughter who had been seduced under promise of marriage by an officer, and had eloped with him from her father's house. They were living together in Lincoln when the officer was forced to go abroad and leave her. He, before he went, boarded her with their landlady, an infamous character, who, to obtain the board she had received in advance without maintaining the unfortunate girl, swore she had robbed her of several articles.

Poor Mary was condemned by her perjury and sentenced to be transported. She had disgraced her friends and dared not apply to them in her distress. She had set the opinions of the world at defiance by her elopement, and there was no one in it who appeared to befriend her, while in all its bitterness she drank the cup of her own mixing. After the departure of the *Lady Julian* her relations had discovered the fate of their lost and ruined Mary. By their exertions the whole scene of the landlady's villainy was exposed, and she stood in the pillory at Lincoln for her perjury.

Upon our arrival we found a pardon lying at Port Jackson, and a chest of excellent clothes sent by the magistrates for her use in the voyage home. She

lodged all the time I was there in the governor's house and every day I took her allowance to her. She was to sail in the first ship for London direct, the *Lady Julian* being bound for China. During the tedious voyage out I took her under my protection. Sarah and she were acquaint before they saw each other in misfortune. Mary washed the clothes and did any little thing for Sarah when she was confined, which she was long before we reached Port Jackson.*

The first place we stopped at was Santa Cruz in the island of Tenerife for water. As we used a great

---

* Mary Rose had the most extraordinary career of any of the convict women mentioned by Nicol. At sixteen she was sentenced to seven years' transportation for stealing clothes. Fortune had smiled upon her, however, in giving her such a romantic and patriotic name. It seems that it never failed to elicit sympathy in her hour of need. Michael Flynn observes that Nicol's view of her 'mixes fact with romantic fiction' but that 'he was not the only one to fall under her spell'.

Following her imprisonment in Lincoln an anonymous poet penned a romantic ballad to publicise her plight. This it seems was associated with a plea for clemency from no less a person than Sir Joseph Banks! Nicol's assertion that a pardon and clothing were waiting for her in Port Jackson is clearly impossible, as no vessel arrived in the settlement from England between the first and second fleets.

Nicol may have been misled by the fact that Governor Phillip was aware of Banks' plea, and arranged for Rose to marry 'one of the best men in this place'. Less than a year later Phillip lamented to Banks that 'my desire of making her better has only been the means of ruining the poor devil who married her'. Rose lived on in Sydney until at least 1825. (See *The Second Fleet*, 508.)

quantity the agent, at the captain's request, had laid
in tea and sugar in place of beef or pork allowed by
government. We boiled a large kettle of water that
served the whole convicts and crew every night and
morning. We allowed them water for washing their
clothes, any quantity they chose, while in port. Many
times they would use four and five boatloads in one
day.

We did not restrain the people on shore from
coming on board through the day. The captains and
seamen who were in port at the time paid us many
visits. Mrs Barnsley bought a cask of wine and got
it on board with the agent's leave. She was very kind
to her fellow convicts who were poor. They were all
anxious to serve her. She was as a queen among
them.

We had a number of Jewesses on board. One,
Sarah Sabolah, had a crucifix, and the others soon got
them and passed themselves for Roman Catholics, by
which means they got many presents from the people
on shore and laid up a large stock for sea.*

We next stood for Sao Tiago, accompanied by two
slave ships from Santa Cruz to Sao Tiago, who sailed
thus far out of their course for the sake of the ladies.
They came on board every day when the weather
would permit. At length they stood for the coast to
pick up their cargo of human misery. We watered

---

* Sarah Sabolah cannot be traced. The name may have been
an assumed one.

again and made all clear for a new start. Our Jewesses played off the same farce with their crucifixes, and with equal success.

We then stood for Rio de Janeiro where we lay eight weeks taking in coffee and sugar, our old stock being now reduced very low. I was employed on shore repairing flour casks to receive it. The Jewesses made here a good harvest, and the ladies had a constant run of visitors. I had received fifty suits of child-bed linen for their use—they were a present from the ladies of England. I here served out twenty suits. Mrs Barnsley acted as midwife and was to practise at Port Jackson, but there was no clergyman on board. When in port the ladies fitted up a kind of tent for themselves.

In crossing the line we had the best sport I ever witnessed upon the same occasion. We had caught a porpoise the day before the ceremony which we skinned to make a dress for Neptune with the tail stuffed. When he came on deck he looked the best representation of a merman I ever saw, painted, with a large swab upon his head for a wig. Not a man in the ship could have known him. One of the convicts fainted, she was so much alarmed at his appearance, and had a miscarriage after. Neptune made the boys confess their amours to him, and I was really astonished at the number. I will not describe the ceremony to fatigue the reader, as it has been often described by others.*

---

* The ceremony of crossing the Equator was an occasion of much merriment. Often the oldest and ugliest sailor was

From Rio de Janeiro we sailed for the Cape of Good Hope, where we took on board seventy-three ewes and a ram for the settlement. We were detained a long time here as we found that the *Guardian* had struck upon an island of ice, and was so severely injured that she was deserted by most of her crew, who were never heard of afterwards. The captain and those who remained with him in the ship were only saved by being towed into the Cape by an American vessel. What detained us was the packing of flour and other necessaries for the colony, as we knew it must be in great want, the *Guardian* being loaded with supplies for it.

At length we sailed for Port Jackson. We made one of the convicts shepherdess, who was so fortunate in her charge of the flock as not to lose one. While we lay at the Cape we had a narrow escape from destruction by fire. The carpenter allowed the pitch-pot to boil over upon the deck, and the flames rose in an alarming manner. The shrieks of the women were dreadful, and the confusion they made running about drove everyone stupid. I ran to my berth, seized a pair of blankets to keep it down until the others drowned it with water. Captain Aitkin made me a handsome present for my exertions.

The captain had a quantity of linen on board, and during the voyage had kept above twenty of the

---

dressed up as King Neptune's wife, and another as Neptune himself. Many liberties were taken with the crew and the officers.

convicts making shirts to sell at Port Jackson. He got them made cheap and sold them to great advantage upon our arrival as the people of the colony were in want of every necessity.

At length, almost to our sorrow, we made the land upon the 3rd of June 1790, just one year all but one day from our leaving the river. We landed all our convicts safe. My charge as steward did not expire for six weeks after our arrival, as the captain, by agreement, was bound to victual them during that time.

It is a fine country and everything thrives well in it. A sergeant of marines supplied the *Lady Julian* with potatoes and garden stuffs for half a crown a day. There were thirty-six people on board and we had as much as we could use. There were only two natives in the town at the time, a boy and a girl.* These had been brought in by a party of the settlers, having been left by their parents. I saw but little of the colony, as my time was fully occupied in my duties as steward, and any moments I could spare I gave them to Sarah.

The days flew on eagles' wings, for we dreaded the hour of separation which at length arrived. It was not without the aid of the military we were brought on board. I offered to lose my wages but we were short of hands, one man having been left sick at Rio de Janeiro, and we had lost our carpenter

* They were Abaroo and Nanbaree, survivors of the smallpox epidemic, who were then living with Surgeon White (Nanbaree) and the Reverend and Mrs Johnson (Abaroo).

who fell overboard. The captain could not spare a man and requested the aid of the governor. I thus was forced to leave Sarah, but we exchanged faith. She promised to remain true, and I promised to return when her time expired and bring her back to England.*

I wished to have stolen her away, but this was impossible, the convicts were so strictly guarded by the marines. There were no soldiers in the colony at this time. With a heavy heart I bade adieu to Port Jackson, resolved to return as soon as I reached England. We would have remained some time longer, but Captain Aitkin was very unwell and the mate was anxious to complete the voyage.

They have an herb in the colony they call sweet tea.** It is infused and drank like the China tea. I liked it much. It requires no sugar and is both a bitter and a sweet. There was an old female convict, her hair quite grey with age, her face shrivelled, who was suckling a child she had borne in the colony. Everyone went to see her, and I among the rest. It was a strange sight. Her hair was quite white. Her fecundity was ascribed to the sweet tea.

---

*   John Nicol and Sarah Whitlam parted for the last time on 25 July 1790. On 26 July Sarah married John Coen Walsh, a first-fleet convict. She signed the marriage register with a cross. In June 1796 the couple sailed for England via India with their two sons. Walsh was back in Australia by 1801 but there are no further records of Sarah Whitlam.

** *Smilax glyciphylla.*

I brought away with me two bags of it as presents to my friends, but two of our men became very ill of the scurvy and I allowed them the use of it, which soon cured them but reduced my store. When we came to China I showed it to my Chinese friends, and they bought it with avidity and importuned me for it and a quantity of the seed I had likewise preserved. I let them have the seed, and only brought a small quantity of the herb to England.

Upon our arrival at Wampoa I renewed my acquaintance with my Chinese friends, and was as happy as I could be with the thoughts of Sarah's situation upon my mind—but this was the dullest voyage I ever made. I changed my berth in the ship, but all would not do. Everything brought her endearing manners to my recollection. To leave her a convict was a great aggravation to my grief. Had I left her by choice for a voyage I could have thought of her with pleasing regret and anxious hope of seeing her soon. But to leave her exposed to temptation in the very worst company the world could produce was too much to think of with composure. I left with her my Bible, the companion of all my voyages, with our names written in it. She used to read it often, when I never thought of it.

So much did these thoughts prey upon my mind I almost resolved to lose my wages by leaving the *Lady Julian* at Rio or the Cape. But to be so far from home, without one penny in my pocket to pay her passage to England, would have been madness, as I could not

bear the idea of bidding for ever farewell to Scotland, the place where my wanderings were always intended to cease.

I made up my mind to come to England in the *Lady Julian*, and get a berth out the first opportunity, and by that time her term of transportation would be expired. We touched at St Helena on our way to England. When we arrived I was paid off and immediately made every inquiry for a ship for New Holland, but there was none, nor any likely to be soon.

10

Author Engaged on Board a South Sea Whaler—Miscellaneous Occurrences—Grief at the Conduct of Sarah—Seal-Fishing—Sea Lions—Unexpectedly Meets a Countryman at Paita—Transactions There.

THERE WAS A vessel called the *Amelia*, Captain Shiels, fitting out as a south-sea whaler. She belonged to Squire Enderborough, Paul's Wharf, London. I got myself engaged as cooper of her. The whole crew were on shares. I, as cooper, had a larger share than a seaman, but this was not my present aim, neither did I think of gain.

I had all my money secured about my person, sewed into my clothes, ready for a start, and with it to pay the passage of Sarah and my son to England. My intention was, when we arrived at Rio de Janeiro on our return home, to fall sick and endeavour to obtain my share from the captain and allow the vessel to sail without me, or to claim it when I reached England. From Rio I could easily get a ship to the Cape. From the Cape to New South Wales I had the only chance of a vessel. I would have remained until the *Amelia* reached the Cape, but she might not even anchor there. These were my views in entering on board the *Amelia*.

In two months after my leaving the *Lady Julian* I was again at sea in hopes of reaching Port Jackson by some means or other. In our first offset we were stranded upon the Red Sand near the Nore. While we lay in distress, the Deal men came out and wished to make a wreck of us by cutting away our masts.* I, with

* Deal was one of the 'cinque ports' near Dover. The men of Deal were pilots, lifeboat men and smugglers known for 'hovelling', or taking disabled ships.

alacrity, aided the captain and stood guard with a brace of pistols, and threatened to blow out the brains of the first man of them that offered to set his foot upon our deck.

The weather fortunately was moderate. We, having no longboat, carried out our anchor between two boats into deep water, and as the tide flowed we got her off. To my great disappointment we were forced to put back into dock to have her examined by removing the copper sheathing. All the crew left her except myself, as the engagement was broken by our return to dock, and the men would not continue in her as they thought no good would come of the voyage. Her stranding was an omen of her bad luck.

There was no ship in the river for New South Wales, and the Indiamen would not sail until about the month of March. The *Amelia* would still be the first vessel. I had no inducement, therefore, to leave her.

We were soon again ready for sea, and set sail with an entire new crew. The first land we made was the island of Buena Vista which belongs to the Portuguese, where we took in livestock, and salt to salt down our seal skins, then stood for Sao Tiago and took in more livestock; from thence to the Falkland Islands for geese and swine. We next made Staten Island, and passed the Straits of Magellan and Straits le Mair, but did not go through either of them. We doubled the Cape then stood down to our fishing ground which was between latitude 18° and the Line.

We had nothing to do but commence, as we had been busy all the voyage preparing and fitting our tackle. Our boilers were fitted up before we left England as in the south seas the spermaceti is all boiled upon the deck. The boiler is built up with fire brick, and a space left between the lower tier and the deck about nine inches high, quite watertight. When once the fire is kindled, which is never after allowed to go out until the ship is fully fished, the space between the bricks and the deck is kept full of water. There are two plug-holes (one on each side) so that when the water heats and would melt the pitch, upon whatever tack the ship may be, the plug is drawn from the under side and the space immediately filled with cold water from the higher side. Great attention is required to watch the boilers. We do not require to carry out fuel to boil our oil, as the refuse of the oil is used ever after the first fire is kindled.

The ashes of the fire is better than any soap. Let our clothes be ever so black and greasy, as they must be from our employment, one shovel full of ashes in a tub of water will make them as clean as when we bought them.

During the fishing we lived wholly upon turtle and were heartily tired of them. We were very fortunate in our fishing. We caught one whale from which we obtained 125 pounds weight of ambergrease, the largest quantity ever brought to England by one ship.

Upon the fishing ground we found the *Venus*, Captain Coffin. She had taken out convicts to Port

Jackson and there was a convict on board at the time. He had concealed himself in her until she was at sea, and by this means made his escape from the colony. He used to hide himself from me but, the other men assuring him I would not inform, he had the courage to speak to me at length, and inquired if ever I had been at Port Jackson.

I told him I had in the *Lady Julian*. He answered he had seen me there. My heart beat high with anxiety. I feared, yet wished, to hear of Sarah Whitlam.

At length I inquired. How shall I express my grief when informed she had left the colony for Bombay. Thus were my worst fears realised. Unconstant woman! Why doubt my faith? Yet dear, and never to be forgotten, I resolved to follow her to India. I could not speak to him so broke off the conversation for the present and left him in greater despondency than I left Port Jackson. My grief was not then mixed with doubts of her constancy. She had only three years to serve when I left her, and these were not yet expired. How she got away he could not inform me.

Every time we met I renewed my inquiries. He was so uniform in his replies, and assured me of its truth so solemnly, I was forced to believe the unpleasant truth. I inquired for my son John, but he could give me no information to be relied on. He believed she had taken him with her but, as the children are taken from the convicts and maintained at school by the

government, he knew not her son from the others, and did not see her go away.

I now had no inducement to go to Port Jackson and for a few days scarce cared what became of me. My love for her revived stronger at this time than any other since I left her. I even gave her praise for leaving it. She did so to be out of bad company, my mind would whisper, and I resolved to get to Bombay as soon as possible, and endeavour to find her out.

As my usual buoyancy of spirits returned, I pursued my labours with all the ardour of a seaman. After taking a sufficient quantity of spermaceti we stood as far down as latitude 3° to the Island of Lopes where we killed thirty thousand seals.* We had a busy time chasing and killing them. When we had a sufficient number we began to kill sea-lions to get their skins for the ship's use. One of their skins was a sufficient load for two men. We used to stand in a gap of the rocks in the morning and knock them down with our clubs as they approached the sea, then stab them with our long knives.

George Parker our mate made a blow at one and missed him. He made a snap at George and sent his tusk right through his arm, a little above the wrist, and walked away at his leisure with him into the sea, Parker roaring like a bull from the pain and terror. Robert Wyld, perceiving his danger, rushed into the water to rescue him, and was up to the armpits before

* Island of Lopes: Lobos Island in northern Peru.

he succeeded in dispatching the unwieldy monster. He then dragged them both on shore where, with difficulty, the tusk was drawn from between the bones, it was so firmly jammed.

We soon after sailed three degrees to the north of the Line to the River Tambo where we anchored, and the captain ascended the river nine miles in his boat, to which I belonged, to the town of Tambo. We had an American Indian for a pilot. He appeared to worship the alligators as he kept constantly bowing and muttering to them, and a busy time he had of it as they were very numerous.

The governor of the town and people were very kind and civil to us. We remained all night at the governor's house, feasting like kings. Captain Shiels made him a present of some porter and a cheese and a few other things, for which he would have given us as many bullocks as we chose. We only took one which was as much as we could use fresh, there being only sixteen hands in the ship. We watered in the river then crossed the Line to the city of Paita, where we anchored in a beautiful bay, quite land-locked and as smooth as a mill-pond.

We scarcely had made all tight when a boat came alongside, and inquired if there was a Scotchman on board. The captain allowed me to go as I was the only one in the ship. I was conducted to a baker's shop in the town and into an elegant room, where a sickly-looking person, but elegantly dressed, rose and met me, shaked hands, and said, 'How's a' wi' you?'

My ears tingled and my heart leapt for joy to hear the accents of my native tongue so unexpectedly. I looked hard at him but had never seen him before. I thanked him and we sat down together and began a long conversation. We talked of Old Scotland and the talk was all on my side for a long while, he had so many questions to put, and he seemed to devour every word I spoke while joy beamed in his sickly features.

At length I got his own history. He was a native of Inverness and had been bred to the sea and, coming to the West Indies, had engaged in the contraband trade carried on along the Spanish main; had been taken prisoner and carried to Montevideo; from thence to Lima where he had been long in prison and suffered many hardships but, being a Roman Catholic, he was not sent to the mines. He had found means to obtain his liberty and afterwards win the love of a rich Spanish lady who procured him his pardon and afterwards married him. He was now very rich and had a ship of his own, besides immense property, but having fallen sick at Paita he had ordered his vessel to proceed on her voyage and send his servants to carry him overland to Lima. He was expecting them every day.

He treated me nobly and made me a handsome present when he went away, which he did while we lay at Paita. I was astonished at the number of servants and horses that came for him. His saddle would have bought fifty horses. The stirrups were solid gold, and every part was loaded with it. The maker seemed to

have studied more to lay on gold than taste in the ornaments. He made the most enticing offers to induce me to go with him, but Sarah was dearer to me than all the riches in the world.

The governor and people of Paita were so kind to us we passed our time very agreeably. All their houses were open to us. They forced presents of fruit upon us, and gave us as much accadent as we chose to drink.*

The governor treated us with a Spanish play. These entertainments are through the day. During the performance we were served with wine, sweetmeats and fruits, but not understanding the language we paid more attention to the refreshments than the play. The governor was one of the kindest gentlemen I ever saw. He told us he loved the English for their humanity; he had been in the town when Lord Anson plundered it.** Ever since they do not keep their saints and plate in the church, but in the town-house which is no stronger than the church. You may see them carrying it back and forward every day.

The governor was very anxious to learn English. I could buy and sell in Spanish. Upon this account he took great notice of me. I had a Spanish and English dictionary on board. I gave it him, and he made me a

* Accadent: spiritous liquor.
** Admiral Anson sailed upon a voyage around the world in the years 1740–44, during which he plundered Paita but showed the inhabitants great mercy.

handsome present he was so much pleased with it—
and he made rapid progress in his study.

He was the first that told me of the King of
France's death. He said, drawing his hand across his
neck, 'The people have cut the neck of de Roi de
Française.' I understood what he meant, but did not
believe the information.

I wore in general, when ashore, a black jacket with
black horn buttons. A priest I used often to meet at
the governor's took a fancy to the buttons and offered
me any price for them. I soon cut off my buttons, and
gave them to him. I had breeches and vest with the
same buttons; off went they, every one. A Jew would
have counted it a good bargain.

Amidst all their kindness they are very superstitious. I must have lain in the streets all night one
evening I missed the boat, had not a Portuguese who
was with me told them I was an Irishman. 'O bon
Irelandois! O bon Christian!' they cried and made me
welcome, gave me the best in the house, happy to
entertain so good a Christian as an Irishman.

While everything was going on to our wish, and
our ambergrease selling well, we were forced to leave
Paita in great haste. One of our men, getting himself tipsy, told the people openly we were selling
ambergrease and had still a great quantity to sell.
The governor immediately sent for the captain and
informed him of his danger. He himself was not against
the sale but should word reach Lima they would
order a frigate to Paita and make a prize of us. We

were too much afraid of this to tarry longer than get in what supplies we stood in need of, for which the governor would accept no payment.

I went with other two to take leave of the governor. As we proceeded along we saw two ladies swinging in a net, and a female servant keeping it in motion. We stood looking at them a few minutes before they perceived us. As soon as they did they desired the servant to cease, came down and bade us come into the house where they treated us with fruit and wine, and would scarce allow us to go away so soon as we wanted. The ladies here have a pale and sickly look. All their movements are languid. Even the men are far from being active. Everyone moves as if he wished someone to carry him.

11

*Rio de Janeiro—Portuguese
Seamen—Lisbon—Author Arrives in
London—Visits Sarah's Parents—
Enters a Vessel Bound for China—
Anecdote.*

WHEN WE SAILED we had two booms over our stern, and a net made fast to them filled with pumpkins, melons and other vegetables, the gift of these kind Spaniards. We stood direct for Rio de Janeiro, where Captain Shiels intended to remain for some time as he had completed his cargo so soon. He would have lost the bounty had he arrived before the time specified in the act of parliament.

There were a great number of Portuguese vessels lying at Rio de Janeiro at this time. No accounts had been received from Lisbon for six months, and it was believed the French had taken Portugal. I counted every day we remained as so much of my time lost, and wearied very much. At length a ship arrived from Lisbon and all the Portuguese prepared to sail. The governor's linguist came on board the *Amelia* and requested, as a personal favour, that Captain Shiels would allow four of his men to go on board the Commodore to assist in the voyage home, as it would be a winter's passage.

I immediately volunteered. I hoped by this means to reach England sooner and obtain more money for Sarah, as I would receive a full share of the *Amelia* in England the same as if I had continued in her. Had I know the delays, the fatigue and vexations I was to endure from these execrable superstitious Portuguese sailors, I never would have left the *Amelia* for any reward the Commodore could have given me—and he was very kind to us. He knew our value, and his whole reliance was upon us. We were to work the ship, and

fight the ship should an enemy lay us alongside. He had been forty years trading between Lisbon and Rio de Janeiro, and in all that time never had made a winter's voyage.

The Portuguese are the worst sailors in the world in rough or cold weather, and we had plenty of both, but worse than all we had a black fellow of a priest on board to whom the crew paid more attention than the captain. He was for ever ringing his bell for mass and sprinkling holy water upon the men. Whenever it blew harder than ordinary they were sure to run to the quarterdeck to the black priest. We were almost foundered at one time by this unseamanlike conduct. The whole crew ran to the quarterdeck, kneeling down, resigned to their fate, the priest sprinkling holy water most profusely upon them, while we four Englishmen were left to steer the vessel and hand the sails. It required two of the four to steer, so that there were only two to hand the sails. The consequence was she broached to. William Mercer and I ran and cut the foregeers, and allowed the yard to swing. At the same time, the captain, mate and boatswain hauled in the forebrace and she righted in a moment. Had her commons not been very high, she must have filled while she lay upon her beam ends. The sea was all over her deck round the hatch, but so soon as she righted and we were going to make sail the Portuguese left their priest and lent us a hand.

We were wrought almost to death and never could have made out the voyage had we not been well fed

and the captain given us plenty of liquor. The black priest rung his bell at his stated time whatever we were doing, and the Portuguese would run to their berths for their crosses. Often the main tack was left half hauled aboard at the sound of his bell, and the vessel left to drift leeward until prayers were over. As two men could do nothing to the sail when the wind was fresh, after prayers they would return and begin bawling and hauling, calling upon their saints as if they would come to assist.

We were thus almost driven to distraction by them and could scarce keep off our hands from boxing their ears. Many a hearty curse they and their saints got. Then they would run to the captain or priest and make complaint that the Englishmen had cursed Saint Antonio or some other of the saints. I often wondered the captain did not confine the priest to his cabin in foul weather, as he was sure to be busiest then. When they complained, the captain took our part and over-awed the Portuguese, or I really believe they would have thrown us overboard. They often looked at us as if they could have eat us without salt, and told us to our face we were 'star pork', that is, all the same as swine—that we knew nothing of God or the saints.

I showed them my Bible and the names of the saints. They were quite surprised. Had I made another voyage I would have made converts of many of them. I was bald headed and they called me an English padre. Often the bell rang while we were at dinner. They inquired why I would not go to mass. 'I mess

with the Coussinero,' I replied.* They began to think I had the best religion. They seemed to think the foul weather was all upon our account, and the virgin and saints sent it because they employed heretics on board.

We had a supercargo on board as passenger, who had made his fortune in the slave trade and was returning home to Portugal. He took unwell and died. At his funeral there were the following manoeuvres gone through. Everyone had a candle in his hand, and all stood in a double line upon the deck. There were even lanthorns hung over the ship's side to light him to the bottom. The body was carried along the double line, the priest chanting, and every one touched him before he was thrown overboard. The captain requested us to do as the others did. Says Will Mercer, 'Captain, I will throw him overboard for you, if you please.'

At length, after a tedious voyage of three months, I got out of this vile crew. When we reached the Tagus the Portuguese began to quarrel and knock us about.** We stood our ground the best way we could until the captain got five of them sent on shore under a guard of soldiers. We remained at the captain's house until we got our wages. The owners gave us a doubloon a piece over and above our agreement for saving the ship, as the captain did us every justice to the owners at the time, saying, 'If the English were as

* Coussinero: cook.
** The Tagus is the estuary Lisbon is situated on.

150

careful of their souls as they are of their bodies, they would be the best people in the world.'

I had many conversations with the captain concerning the ignorance of the Portuguese people in general, and asked why the priest did not inform them better. He said, 'Were we to inform them they would soon turn the priest about his business and rise against the government. They must only get knowledge little by little.'

We assisted at a religious ceremony before we came away, at the special request of our kind friend the captain. The foresail that was set when she broached to was given as an offering to the church, as the black priest told them it was through it they were saved. Although the worst sailor in the world knew it was the sail that would have sunk us, they dared not contradict the priest. The whole ship's crew carried it through the streets of Lisbon upon handkerchiefs to the church where it was placed upon the altar with much mummery. We came away and left them but the owners of the vessel bought back the sail again, after the priests had blessed it to their minds, as the church had more use for money than foresails.

William Mercer and I entered on board a brig bound for London, which was to sail in a few days, during which time we rambled about through the filthy streets of Lisbon. The higher orders of the Portuguese are very kind and civil. I was too late one evening to get on board the brig. A Portuguese merchant noticed my perplexity, for it is no pleasing thing

to have a lodging to seek in Lisbon at a latish hour. Without my requesting him, he took me to his own house, gave me an excellent supper and bed. Had I been a gentleman of his acquaintance he could not have been kinder or paid me more attention. He ordered his servant to call me at any hour in the morning I chose.

As war was now looked for we were afraid for the press.* The Portuguese captain, at our request, got each of us a protection from the British consul at Lisbon. With a joyful heart I set sail for London to look out for an Indiaman that I might get to Bombay and inquire for Sarah, for she was still the idol of all my affections. At this time I was all anxiety to reach England. I often hoped she had reached her father's house and there was pining at my absence. I used for days to flatter myself with these dreams.

When we arrived at Gravesend a man-of-war's boat came on board to press any Englishmen there might be on board. William and I did not choose to trust to our protections now that we were in the river. So we stowed ourselves away among some bags of cotton where we were almost smothered but could hear every word that was said. The captain told the lieutenant he had no more hands than he saw, and they were all Portuguese. The lieutenant was not very particular, and left the brig without making much search.

* Britain had by now entered the French Revolutionary Wars.

When the boat left the vessel we crept from our hiding hole, and not long after a custom-house officer came on board. When we cast anchor, as I had a suit of long clothes in my chest that I had provided, should I have been so fortunate as have found Sarah at Port Jackson, to dash away with her a bit on shore, I put them on immediately and gave the custom-house officer half a guinea for the loan of his cocked hat and powdered wig. The long gilt-headed cane was included in the bargain.

I got a waterman to put me on shore. I am confident my own father, had he been alive, could not have known me with my cane in my hand, cocked hat and bushy wig. I inquired at the waterman the way to the inn where the coach set out from for London; I at the same time knew as well as him. I passed for a passenger. At the inn I called for a pint of wine, pens and ink, and was busy writing any nonsense that came in my head until the coach set off. All these precautions were necessary. Had the waterman suspected me to be a sailor he would have informed the press-gang in one minute. The waiters at the inn would have done the same.

By these precautions I arrived safe in London but did not go down to Wapping until next day, where I took up my old lodgings, still in my disguise. My landlord went on board and brought on shore my bedding and chest. I left them under his charge while I went to Lincoln to Sarah's parents where I made every inquiry—but they knew not so much of her as I did

myself. The last information they had obtained was from the letter I had put in the post office for them before I sailed in the *Amelia*.

I immediately returned to London where, to my disappointment, I found there was not a berth to be got in any of the Indiamen who were for Bombay direct. They were all full. I then, as my next best, went to be engaged as cooper on board the *Nottingham* for China direct, depending on providence if we were ever to meet again. To find some way to effect my purpose, my landlord took me to be impressed. He got the six guineas allowed the bringer, which he returned to me. He was from Inverness, as honest a man as ever lived. I had always boarded in his house when in London.

A curious scene happened at my entry. There were a few more impressed on the same day, one an old tar. When asked by Captain Rogers, in his examination, how they hauled the main tack aboard, he replied, 'I can't tell, your honour, but I can show.' He clapped his foot into Captain Rogers' pocket, at the same instant leaped on his shoulders, tore his coat to the skirts, saying, 'Thus we haul it aboard.'

Captain Barefoot of the *Nottingham* and the other captains laughed heartily, as well as Rogers, who said rather peevishly, 'You might have shown, without tearing my coat.'

'How could I, your honour?' was the reply.*

* Perhaps this was the only means the old tar had of showing his displeasure at being pressed.

12

Arrival at the Cape of Good Hope—
Singular Incident—Java—
Wampoa—Chinese Artificers—
Music—Returns to England, and is
Impressed—Leith Roads—Mutiny—
Storm at Sea.

I THUS AGAIN set off as cooper of the *Not-tingham* in 1793. Nothing worthy of notice happened. As I have gone over the same voyage before I will not detain the reader, but one circumstance that I witnessed off the Cape of Good Hope I cannot avoid mentioning as a dreadful example of what man will dare, and the perils he will encounter, to free himself from a situation he dislikes.

A man-of-war had been washing her gratings when the India fleet hove in sight. (They are washed by being lowered overboard and allowed to float astern.) Four or five men had slipped down upon them, cut them adrift and were thus voluntarily committed to the vast Atlantic without a bit of biscuit or a drop of water or any means of guiding the gratings they were floating upon in the hope of being picked up by some vessel. They held out their arms to us and supplicated in the wildest manner to be taken on board.

The captain would not. The *Nottingham* was a fast sailing ship and the first in the fleet. He said, 'I will not. Some of the stern ships will pick them up.' While he spoke these unfortunate and desponding fellow creatures lessened to our view, while their cries rung in our ears. I hope some of the stern ships picked them up. Few things I have seen are more strongly impressed upon my memory than the despairing looks and frantic gestures of these victims in quest of liberty. Next morning the frigate they had left came alongside of us and inquired if we had seen them. The captain gave an indirect answer to their inquiries, as well he might.

When we arrived at Java and anchored at Batavia
I made every inquiry for a country ship, and would
have left the *Nottingham* in a moment had there been
one.* All my money was concealed upon my person
for a start. I thought of falling sick and remaining until
a country ship came, but I might really have become
what I feigned in this European's grave, as I must have
remained in the hospital. Had I walked about the city
in health, the Dutch would soon have kidnapped me.
I was thus once more baffled.

Indeed, I must confess, I did not feel the same
anguish now I had endured before. It was now four
years since I had left her in the colony, and her leaving
it so soon, without waiting for me, showed she cared
less about me than I cared for her. Not to write to
her parents I had often thought very neglectful of her.
I made up my mind not to leave the *Nottingham* at
such risks, but to return in her to England and settle,
as I had now some cash and had seen all I could see,
and just make one more call at her friends in Lincoln,
in my way to Scotland, and be ruled by the information
tion I there obtained.

We sailed for Wampoa, where I was kindly
received by my Chinese friends. I now paid more
attention and saw things without the glare of novelty
and have no cause to alter anything I said before. I
had always, while at home, thought them the best
tradesmen and most ingenious of people. I am

* Batavia: Jakarta.

inclined to think they have been overrated in regard to their abilities. Some things they do very neat, but considering the things they have to do them with it is no wonder. I mean their varnishes and colours, native productions.

Let the following facts that I can vouch for speak for themselves. In my own line they are unable to make any article with two ends, such as barrels. They have only reached the length of a tub. These they dool, that is pin with bamboos, the joints of the staves as well as the bottom. When a cask that comes from Europe is to be broached they cannot even bore and place the crane on it. A foreign cooper must go on shore and do it. Many a half dollar I have got for this service myself from the Chinese merchants.

I do not believe they can make a nail with a head. Many thousand of their nails I have had through my hands, and never saw one with a head upon it such as we have in England. Their nails are either sprigs or simply bent like a crow's toe. They are the worst smiths of any people, and can do nothing with a bar of iron if thick. I and the other coopers always kept the cuttings of our hoops which they bought with avidity—but larger pieces they would scarce take from us.

A vessel, the *Argyll*, while we were there in the *King George*, had lost her rudder in the voyage out and could not sail without a new one. There was not a smith in Canton who could forge the ironwork. The captain of the ship applied to the armourer of the *King*

George who took it in hand and in three weeks gained one hundred dollars by the job.

They appear to me to be excellent copiers, but not inventors. One of our officers sat for a painter to draw his picture and told the Chinese not to make him ugly. 'How can make other than is?' was the reply. He had no idea of altering a single feature to add to the looks of the object he was painting. All was a slavish copy of what was before his eyes. If you want anything made out of the common they must have one of the same as a pattern or they will not take it in hand. And what is further proof of their want of invention is, when you see one house you have seen every house of the same rank, or any other articles of their manufacture you have seen all. There is scarcely any variety and you need give yourself no trouble looking for others if the price pleases.

There is no change of fashion: the oldest articles you can fall in with are the same make and fashion as the newest, and a traveller who visited the country two hundred years ago could know no difference but in the men. They would be new, the old having died; the present race, I may say, wearing their dress and inhabiting their houses without the least change in the general appearance.

The only instrument of music I saw was a bagpipe, like the small Lowland pipe, on which they play well. Their gongs cannot be called a musical instrument. When John Tuck, the deputy emperor, appears (he is called so by the seamen on account of his having a

gallows on board the grand boat which is as large as a seventy-four-gun ship and crowded with attendants), his band consists only of bagpipes. Their gongs are only used that I heard to make *tchin, tchin* to Joss in bad weather and at their paper sacrifices; and every vessel, down to the smallest sampan, has a Joss on board.

The deputy emperor comes once every year to view the fleet and pay his respects to the commodore. It is the grandest sight upon the river. Not so much as a sampan is allowed to move. He makes a present to every ship in the fleet of bullocks, wine, schamsee and flour. The officers start the schamsee overboard— it is a pernicious liquor distilled from rice. The flour is so coarse it is given to the hogs.

They measure every ship and can tell to a quarter chest how much she will hold. The first American sloop that came, she having only one mast, the Chinamen said, 'Hey, yaw, what fashion? How can measure ship with one mast?'—they having been accustomed to measure ships with more masts than one. They measure between the masts the breadth and depth of the ship.

I went up the river to the Dutch Folly, a fort lying waste opposite Canton in the middle of the river. The Dutch pretended they wished to build an hospital for their sick and got leave to do so, but their design was discovered by the bursting of a large barrel full of shot, and the Chinese put a stop to their undertaking, which now lies waste.

The Chinese sell all their fish, frogs, rats and hogs alive, and all by weight. Their frogs are bred and fed by them and are the largest I ever saw. When we bought our sea stock the hogs came on board in the baskets in which they were weighed.

The Chinese women are seldom seen in the streets. They walk very ill, and their gowns sweep the ground. Their hair is very prettily done up in the form of a crown on the top of their heads and fastened with a large gold or silver pin. The Tartar women are to be met at every step.

The cargo being complete, we fell down the river using our old precaution to keep off the Chinese chop-officers, and they retired with the same exclamation, 'Hey, yaw, what fashion? Too much baubry. Too much baubry.'

Nothing uncommon happened until we reached the Downs. I had allowed my beard to grow long and myself to be very dirty to be as unlikely as possible when the man-of-war boats came on board to press the crew. As we expected, they came. I was in the hold, sorting among the water casks, and escaped. They took every hand that would answer. I rejoiced in my escape but my joy was of short duration. One of the men they had taken had a sore leg. The boat brought him back—and I had the bad luck to be taken and he was left. Thus were all my schemes blown into the air.

I found myself in a situation I could not leave, a bondage that had been imposed upon me against my

will, and no hopes of relief until the end of the war—
not that I disliked it, but I had now become weary of
wandering for a time and longed to see Scotland
again. My heart always pointed to my native land.
Remonstrance and complaint were equally vain.

I therefore made up my mind to it, and was as
happy as a man in blasted prospects can be. I was
taken on board the *Venerable*, Admiral Duncan. She
was the flagship and commanded by Captain Hope,
now Admiral Hope. The *Venerable's* boats had made
a clean ship of the *Nottingham*. She was forced to be
brought up the river by ticket-porters and old Greenwich men. Next morning sixty of us who had
belonged to the *Nottingham* were turned over to the
Edgar, seventy-four, Captain Sir Charles Henry
Knowles. This was on the 11th June 1794. I was
stationed in the gunner's crew.

We went upon a cruise to the coast of Norway,
then touched at Shetland for fresh provisions. Afterwards we sailed for Leith Roads. I now felt all the
inconveniencies of my confinement. I was at home in
sight of the place where I wished all my wanderings
to cease. Captain Barefoot of the *Nottingham* had
wrote to Sir C. H. Knowles in my behalf, and he was
very kind to me. I asked leave to go on shore to see
my friends which he consented to, but Lieutenant
Collis would not allow me, saying 'it was not safe to
allow a pressed man to go on shore at his native place'.

Had I been allowed, I did not intend to leave the
Edgar. I would not have run away for any money,

upon my kind captain's account. My uncle came on board and saw me before we sailed, and I was visited by my other friends, which made me quite happy.

While we lay in Leith Roads, a mutiny broke out in the *Defiance*, seventy-four. The cause was, their captain gave them five-water grog; now the common thing is three-waters. The weather was cold. The spirit thus reduced was, as the mutineers called it, as thin as muslin and quite unfit to keep out the cold. No seaman could endure this in cold climates. Had they been in hot latitudes they would have been happy to get it thus for the sake of the water, but then they would not have got it.

The *Edgar* was ordered alongside the *Defiance* to engage her, if necessary, to bring her to order. We were saved this dreadful alternative by their returning to duty. She was manned principally by fishermen, stout resolute dogs. When bearing down upon her my heart felt so sad and heavy, not that I feared death or wounds, but to fight my brother, as it were. I do not believe the *Edgar's* crew would have manned the guns. They thought the *Defiance* men were in the right, and had they engaged us heartily as we would have done a French seventy-four, we could have done no good, only blown each other out of the water, for the ships were of equal force; and if there were any odds the *Defiance* had it in point of crew. Had I received my discharge and one hundred guineas I could not have felt my heart lighter than I did when we returned to our anchorage. And the gloom immediately vanished from every face in the ship.

We shortly after sailed on a cruise in the north seas and encountered a dreadful gale on the 17th October. I never was in such danger in all my life. The *Edgar* was only newly put in commission, and her rigging was new and not properly seasoned. We in a few hours carried away our bowsprit and foremast in this dreadful night, then our mizen and main topmast. With great difficulty we cut them clear. Soon after our mainmast loosened in the step, and we every moment expected it to go through her bottom. Then no exertion could have saved us from destruction. The carpenter, by good fortune, got it secured.

We lost all our anchors and cables in our attempts to bring her to, save one. At length it moderated a little, when we rigged jury masts and made for the Humber where we brought to with our only remaining anchor—when the *Inflexible*, Captain Savage, hove in sight and took us in tow. When in this situation the coasters, as they passed, called to the *Inflexible*, 'What prize have you got in tow?' A fresh gale sprung up and the *Inflexible* was forced to cast us off.

The weather moderated again and we proceeded up the Swain the best way we could into Blackstakes, Chatham. My berth during the storm, as one of the gunner's crew, was in charge of the powder on deck we used in firing our guns of distress. The ship rolled so much we were often upon our beam ends, and rolled a number of our guns overboard. We were forced to start all our beer and water to lighten the ship, but we rode it out, contrary to our expectation,

and were shortly after turned over, captain and all, to the *Goliah*, seventy-four guns, and sailed to join Sir John Jervis in the blockade of Toulon. We boarded a Spanish ship and found on board thirty Austrian prisoners. They every man entered with us as marines.

13

*Action off Cape St Vincent—
Blockade of Cadiz—Action at
Aboukir Bay—Anecdotes of the
Battle—Subsequent Occurrences—
Landing of the British Army in
Egypt—Ophthalmia—Return to
England.*

W E NEXT SAILED for St Forensa Bay in the island of Corsica to water, but found the French in possession of the watering-place, and could get none. I belonged to the launch and had charge of the powder and match. I was constantly on shore when any service was to be done in destroying stores, spiking guns, blowing up batteries, and enjoyed it much. We carried off all the brass guns, and those metal ones that were near the edge of the rocks we threw into the sea. This was excellent sport to us but we were forced to leave it and sail to Gibraltar for water and provisions; but could obtain no supplies and sailed for Lisbon where we got plenty, having been on short allowance for some time before.

While we lay at Lisbon we got private intelligence overland that the Spanish fleet was at sea. We with all dispatch set sail in pursuit of them. We were so fortunate as come in sight of them by break of day, on the 14th of February, off Cape St Vincent. They consisted of twenty-five sail, mostly three-deckers. We were only eighteen but we were English, and we gave them their valentines in style.

Soon as we came in sight, a bustle commenced not to be conceived or described. To do it justice, while every man was as busy as he could be the greater order prevailed. A serious cast was to be perceived on every face but not a shade of doubt or fear. We rejoiced in a general action; not that we loved fighting, but we all wished to be free to return to our homes and follow our own pursuits. We knew there was no other way

of obtaining this than by defeating the enemy. 'The hotter war the sooner peace,' was a saying with us. When everything was cleared, the ports open, the matches lighted and guns run out, then we gave them three such cheers as are only to be heard in a British man-of-war. This intimidates the enemy more than a broadside, as they have often declared to me. It shows them all is right, and the men in the true spirit baying to be at them.

During the action, my situation was not one of danger but most wounding to my feelings and trying to my patience. I was stationed in the after-magazine, serving powder from the screen, and could see nothing—but I could feel every shot that struck the *Goliah*, and the cries and groans of the wounded were most distressing as there was only the thickness of the blankets of the screen between me and them. Busy as I was, the time hung upon me with a dreary weight. Not a soul spoke to me but the master-at-arms as he went his rounds to inquire if all was safe. No sick person ever longed more for his physician than I for the voice of the master-at-arms. The surgeon's-mate at the commencement of the action spoke a little, but his hands were soon too full of his own affairs.

Those who were carrying run like wild creatures and scarce opened their lips. I would far rather have been on the decks amid the bustle, for there the time flew on eagle's wings. The *Goliah* was sore beset; for some time she had two three-deckers upon her. The men stood to their guns as cool as if they had been

exercising. The admiral ordered the *Britannia* to our assistance. Iron-sides, with her forty-twos, soon made them sheer off.† Towards the close of the action the men were very weary. One lad put his head out of the porthole, saying, 'Damn them, are they not going to strike yet?' For us to strike was out of the question.

At length the roar of the guns ceased and I came on deck to see the effects of a great sea engagement— but such a scene of blood and desolation I want words to express. I had been in a great number of actions with single ships in the *Proteus* and *Surprise* during the seven years I was in them. This was my first action in a fleet and I had only a small share in it. We had destroyed a great number and secured four three-deckers. One they had the impiety to call the *Holy Ghost* we wished much to get, but they towed her off. The fleet was in such a shattered situation we lay twenty-four hours in sight of them, repairing our rigging.

It is after the action the disagreeable part commences. The crews are wrought to the utmost of their strength. For days they have no remission of their toil, repairing the rigging and other parts injured in the action. Their spirits are broke by fatigue. They have no leisure to talk of the battle and, when the usual

---

† The *Britannia* is a first-rate, carrying 110 guns. She was the only ship that carried forty-two-pounders on her lower deck, and thirty-two on her middle deck. She was the strongest built ship in the navy. The sailors upon this account called her 'Iron-Sides'.

round of duty returns, we do not choose to revert to a disagreeable subject. Who can speak of what he did where all did their utmost? One of my mess-mates had the heel of his shoe shot off. The skin was not broke yet his leg swelled and became black. He was lame for a long time.

On our return to Lisbon we lost one of the fleet, the *Bombay Castle*. She was stranded and completely lost. All her crew were saved. We were in great danger in the *Goliah*. Captain Sir C. H. Knowles was tried for not lending assistance, when he needed it himself. The court-martial honourably acquitted him. Collis, our first lieutenant, told us not to cheer when he came on board, but we loved our captain too well to be restrained. We had agreed upon a signal with the cox-swain, if he was, as he ought to be, honourably acquit-ted. The signal was given and in vain Collis forbade. We manned the yards and gave three hearty cheers. Not a man on board but would have bled for Sir C. H. Knowles. To our regret we lost him to our ship at this very time. He was as good a captain as I ever sailed with. He was made admiral, and went home in the *Britannia*.

Captain Foley took command of the *Goliah* and we joined the blockade of Cadiz where we remained, sending our boat to assist at the bombardments and covering them, until Admiral Nelson came out again and picked out thirteen seventy-fours from the fleet. The *Goliah* was one. She was the fastest sailing ship in the fleet. We did not stay to water but got a supply

from the ships that were to remain, and away we set under a press of sail, not knowing where.

We came to an anchor in the Straits of Messina. There was an American man-of-war at anchor. Captain Foley ordered him to unmoor that the *Goliah* might get her station, as it was a good one near the shore, but Jonathan would not budge, but made answer, 'I will let you know I belong to the United States of America and I will not give way to any nation under the sun but in a good cause.'*

So we came to an anchor where we could. We remained here but a short time when we got intelligence that the French fleet were up the Straits. We then made sail for Egypt but missed them, and came back to Syracuse and watered in twenty-four hours. I was up all night filling water. The day after we left Syracuse we fell in with a French brig who had just left the fleet. Admiral Nelson took her in tow and she conducted us to where they lay at anchor in Aboukir Bay.**

We had our anchors out at our stern port with a spring upon them, and the cable carried along the ship's side, so that the anchors were at our bows, as if there was no change in the arrangement. This was to prevent the ships from swinging round, as every ship was to be brought to by her stern. We ran in between the French fleet and the shore to prevent any

* Jonathan: A generic name for an American.
** Aboukir Bay: near Alexandria in Egypt.

communication between the enemy and the shore. Soon as they were in sight a signal was made from the admiral's ship for every vessel as she came up to make the best of her way, firing upon the French ships as she passed, and 'every man to take his bird' as we joking called it.

The *Goliah* led the van. There was a French frigate right in our way. Captain Foley cried, 'Sink that brute, what does he there?' In a moment she went to the bottom and her crew were seen running into her rigging. The sun was just setting as we went into the bay, and a red and fiery sun it was. I would, if had I had my choice, been on the deck. There I would have seen what was passing and the time would not have hung so heavy, but every man does his duty with spirit, whether his station be in the slaughterhouse or the magazine.†

I saw as little of this action as I did of the one on the 14th February off Cape St Vincent. My station was in the powder magazine with the gunner. As we entered the bay we stripped to our trousers, opened our ports, cleared, and every ship we passed gave them a broadside and three cheers. Any information we got was from the boys and women who carried the powder. The women behaved as well as the men, and got a present for their bravery from the grand signior.

† The seamen call the lower deck near the mainmast the slaughterhouse, as it is amidships and the enemy aim their fire principally at the body of the ship.

When the French admiral's ship blew up, the *Goliah* got such a shake we thought the after-part of her had blown up until the boys told us what it was. They brought us every now and then the cheering news of another French ship having struck, and we answered the cheers on deck with heartfelt joy. In the heat of the action a shot came right into the magazine but did no harm as the carpenters plugged it up and stopped the water that was rushing in.

I was much indebted to the gunner's wife who gave her husband and me a drink of wine every now and then, which lessened our fatigue much. There were some of the women wounded, and one woman belonging to Leith died of her wounds and was buried on a small island in the bay. One woman bore a son in the heat of the action. She belonged to Edinburgh.

When we ceased firing I went on deck to view the state of the fleets, and an awful sight it was. The whole bay was covered with dead bodies, mangled, wounded and scorched, not a bit of clothes on them except their trousers. There were a number of French, belonging to the French admiral's ship the *L'Orient*, who had swam to the *Goliah* and were cowering under her forecastle. Poor fellows, they were brought on board and Captain Foley ordered them down to the steward's room to get provisions and clothing.

One thing I observed in these Frenchmen quite different from anything I had ever before observed. In the American war, when we took a French ship, the *Duke de Chartres*, the prisoners were as merry as

if they had taken us, only saying, '*Fortune de guerre*'—
you take me today, I take you tomorrow. Those we
now had on board were thankful for our kindness but
were sullen and as downcast as if each had lost a ship
of his own.

The only incidents I heard of are two. One lad who
was stationed by a salt box on which he sat to give out
cartridges and keep the lid close—it is a trying
berth—when asked for a cartridge, he gave none, yet
he sat upright. His eyes were open. One of the men
gave him a push. He fell all his length on the deck.
There was not a blemish on his body yet he was quite
dead, and was thrown overboard. The other, a lad
who had the match in his hand to fire his gun. In the
act of applying it a shot took off his arm. It hung by
a small piece of skin. The match fell to the deck. He
looked to his arm and, seeing what had happened,
seized the match in his left hand and fired off the gun
before he went to the cockpit to have it dressed. They
were in our mess or I might never have heard of it.
Two of the mess were killed and I knew not of it until
the day after. Thus terminated the glorious first of
August, the busiest night in my life.

Soon after the action the whole fleet set sail with
the prizes, and left the *Goliah* as guard ship. We
remained here until we were relieved by the *Tigre*,
seventy-four, when we sailed for Naples to refit. After
refitting we sailed for Malta to join in the blockade,
where we remained eight months without any occurrence worthy of notice. At length the *Goliah* became

so leaky we were forced to leave our station and sail for Gibraltar where, after watering, we sailed for England.

We got some marines from the Rock to reinforce the *Goliah's* complement—one of them a tall stout Englishman who had been cock of the Rock.* He was very overbearing. There are often quarrels at the ship's fires when the men are boiling their kettles. We had a stout little fellow of an Irishman, who had been long in the *Goliah*. The marine pushed his kettle aside. Paddy demanded why he did so.

'Because I choose to do it.'

'I won't allow you while the life is in me,' was the reply.

'Do you wish to fight?' said the Englishman.

'Yes, and I do,' said Paddy. 'I will take the Gibraltar rust out of you or you shall beat the life out of my body before we are done.'

A fight was made up in a minute, and they went well forward on the deck to be out of sight of the officers. To it they went and fought it out, we forming a ring and screening them from observation. Paddy was as good as his word, for he took the rust off the marine so well he was forced to give in, and we were all happy to see the lobster-back's pride taken out of him.

On our arrival she was put out of commission, and the crew turned over to the *Royal William*, the guard

* The Rock: Gibraltar.

ship, and had two or three days' liberty on shore by the admiral's order.

I was next drafted on board the *Ramilies* and sailed for Belleisle, but remained only a short time in her when I was turned over to the *Ajax*, Captain Alexander F. Cochrane, upon preferment.* We sailed for Ferrol and attempted to cut out some vessels but did not succeed, then stood for Algiers to water, having a fleet of transports with troops on board under convoy. The troops were commanded by Sir Ralph Abercromby. Having watered, we sailed with the army to Mamarice Bay, and the troops were encamped upon a fine piece of ground, with a rivulet running through the centre. The French had just left the place, having first done all the mischief in their power.

While we lay here an engineer named William Balcarras went in a frigate to reconnoitre the French works. He landed and, having attained his object, was coming off in his boat when he was followed by another from the shore and shot dead before he reached the frigate.

We left Mamarice Bay and sailed to Rhodes, where we took in forage for the cavalry. We then sailed for Alexandria and landed the troops.

I belonged to one of the boats. Captain A. F. Cochrane was beach-master, and had the ordering of the troops in the landing. We began to leave the ships about twelve o'clock and reached the shore about

* Belleisle is in the Bay of Biscay.

sunrise in the morning. We rowed very slow with our oars muffled. It was a pleasant night. The water was very still and all was as silent as death. No one spoke but each cast an anxious look to the shore, then at each other, impatient to land. Each boat carried about one hundred men and did not draw nine inches of water.

The French cavalry were ready to receive us, but we soon forced them back and landed eight thousand men the first morning. We had good sport at landing the troops as the Frenchmen made a stout resistance. We brought back the wounded men to the ships.

For some time we supplied the troops on shore with provisions and water. After the advance of the troops into the country I was with the seamen on shore, assisting at the siege of Alexandria and working like a labourer in cutting off the branch of the Nile that supplied the city with water. One of the *Ajax's* boats, at Sir Ralph Abercromby's request, carried him after receiving his wound, on board the hospital ship.

Of all the countries I was ever in, in all my wanderings, I could not remain in Egypt. The air is so dry and I felt so disagreeable. It is, on the whole, sandy and barren, yet what I saw of it that was cultivated is very agreeable. For some days before the town surrendered I had been so bad with the flux I was forced to go on board. After the town surrendered and the operations of the army ceased we sailed for Malta. At this time I was blind with the ophthalmia and continued thus for six weeks.

My sufferings were most acute. I could not lie down for a moment, for the scalding water that continually flowed from my eyes filled them and put me to exquisite torture. I sat constantly on my chest with a vessel of cold water bathing them. If I slept I awoke in an agony of pain. All the time the flux was most severe upon me and the surgeon would not dry it up, as it, he said, relieved my eyes. When we came to Malta a French surgeon cured me by touching the balls of my eyes with tincture of opium, but the pain of the application was very severe. Thank God, however, I soon after recovered my health and spirits.

From Malta we sailed to Gibraltar where we watered, then sailed for England where, to my joy, I found that peace was concluded. We were all paid off shortly after our arrival. I was ship's corporal when I was discharged.

14

*Author Arrives in Edinburgh—
Marries and Settles as a Cooper—
Forced to Leave his Business from
Danger of Impressment—Retires to
Cousland—Subsequent
Occurrences—Returns to Edinburgh
from Inability to Work at
Cousland—Failure of Prospects—
Present Situation.*

I WAS ONCE more my own master, and felt so happy I was like one bewildered. Did those on shore only experience half the sensations of a sailor at perfect liberty after being seven years on board ship without a will of his own, they would not blame his eccentricities but wonder he was not more foolish.

After a few days my cooler reason began to resume its power and I began to think what should be my after pursuits. It was now seven years since I had been pressed from the *Nottingham*. In that time the thoughts of Sarah had faded into a distant pleasing dream. The violent desire I at one time felt to repossess her was now softened into a curiosity to know what had become of her.

As I was now possessed of a good deal of pay and prize-money due, when I received it I went down by Lincoln to make inquiry, but no one had heard of her since I was there myself, nine years before. So all my inquiries after her terminated and I proceeded to Scotland, determined to settle, as I was now too old to undertake any more love pilgrimages after an individual, as I knew not in what quarter of the globe she was or whether she was dead or alive.

I arrived in Edinburgh just twenty-five years after I had left it to wander over the globe. I had been only twice there, once at the end of the American war when I found my father dead and my brothers wanderers. After my return from the voyage with Captain Portlock I remained only a few days and just passed through the city. When in the *Edgar*, I never had been on shore.

I scarce knew a face in Edinburgh. It had doubled itself in my absence. I now wandered in elegant streets where I had left corn growing. Everything was new to me. I confess I felt more sincere pleasure and enjoyment in beholding the beauties of Edinburgh than ever I felt in any foreign clime, for I now could identify myself with them. I was a Scotchman and I felt as if they were my own property. In China, in Naples, in Rio de Janeiro or even in London I felt as a stranger, and I beheld with only the eye of curiosity.

Here I now looked on with the eye of a son who is witnessing the improvements of his father's house. Little did I at this time think I should wander in these very streets to pick up a few coals to warm my aged limbs! But everything is wisely ordered by that Power who has protected me in dangers when I thought not of Him.

I felt myself, for a few weeks after my arrival, not so very happy. As I had anticipated, there was scarcely a friend I had left that I knew again. The old were dead, the young had grown up to manhood and many were in foreign climes. The Firth of Forth which in my youth appeared a sea to my inexperienced mind, Arthur Seat and the neighbouring hills, now seemed dwindled to insignificance in comparison to what I had witnessed in foreign parts. Because they were my native scenery I felt hurt that any other country should possess more imposing objects of their kind. But they were Scotch and I loved them still.

I could not settle to work but wandered up and

down. At length I fell in with a cousin of my own. We had been playfellows and a friendly intimacy had continued until I went to sea. I fixed my affections on her and we were married. I gave her my solemn promise never again to go to sea during her life. I then thought sincerely of settling and following my trade. I bought a house in the Castle Hill and furnished it well, then laid in a stock of wood and tools. I had as much work as I could do for a soap work at the Queensferry. For one year my prospects were as good as I could have wished, and I was as happy as ever I had been in my life.

But in a few months after the war broke out again and the press-gang came in quest of me.* I could no longer remain in Edinburgh and avoid them. My wife was like a distracted woman and gave me no rest until I sold off my stock in trade and the greater part of my furniture and retired to the country. Even until I got this accomplished I dared not to sleep in my own house, as I had more than one call from the gang.

I went to Cousland, nine miles from Edinburgh in the parish of Cranstoun, and put up at one Robert Moodie's, a small public house, not knowing what was to be my next pursuit. I could obtain no employment as a cooper unless I lived in a large or seaport town, and there I could not remain. I at length applied to Mr Dickson and got work from him at the lime quarries. My berth was to bore and charge the stones with

---

* Britain had entered the Napoleonic Wars.

gunpowder to facilitate the work. I continued to live at Robert Moodie's, my wife Margaret paying me an occasional visit, until I got a house of my own from Mr Dickson, when she came out to reside constantly with me.

I hoped that every month would put a period to the war and I would be allowed to return to Edinburgh. But peace still seemed to recede from Britain. Year after year I looked for it in vain. When the weather was good, night after night have I sat after my day's labour by the old windmill in Bartholomew's field, first gazing upon Edinburgh that I dared not reside in, then upon the vessels that glided along the Forth. A sigh would escape me at my present lot. My promise to Margaret kept me from them (my word has ever been my bond) or I should assuredly have gone to sea again. I was like a bird in a cage, with objects that I desired on every side but could not obtain.

The cultivation of the small garden attached to my cottage occupied my mind for some time. I was becoming a little more reconciled to my lot when the press-gang came out even to Cousland and took away a neighbour of the name of Murray. He had a large family and, through the interest of the minister and neighbouring gentlemen, he got off. His impressment was a great blow to my tranquillity for many months. For a long time I slept every night either in Dalkeith or Musselburgh, and during the day a stranger could not appear near the quarry without causing the most

disagreeable sensations to me. At length this cause of
uneasiness wore off likewise, and I settled down to my
usual calm expectations of peace—but year followed
year and my prospects were unaltered.

I now began to see the great alterations that had
taken place in the country from the time I had been
in it, when a boy, about the year 1766. At that time I
had resided for some time with my uncle at Edmonstone. The country was very little inclosed. The
farmers lived with their servants. Now the country
was inclosed and the farmers were gentlemen.*

At Dalkeith fair, when the crops were off the
ground, it was called 'long halter time'. The cattle
during the fair got leave to stray at large while the
farmers, their wives, daughters and servants were all
at the fair, only one woman being left at home. Now
the farmers, if they went to the fair, it was to sell or
buy, not to make merry. Their wives and daughters
would have thought themselves disgraced if they were
seen at the fair. They no longer messed with their
servants but lived like noblemen by themselves. If a
servant had occasion to speak to his master, he must
address him as if he had been an admiral—this to me
appeared strange at first.

As Mr Dickson knew I was anxious for the news,
he was so kind as give me a reading of the newspapers
when he was done. The other workmen assembled in

* Inclosing was the annexing of common fields, meadows and
  pastures into consolidated farms.

my cottage on the evenings I got them and I read aloud. Then we would discuss the important parts together. The others were not friendly to the government, save one, an old soldier who had been in the East Indies. He and I always sided together. I had broke His Majesty's bread for fourteen years and would not, upon that account, hear his government spoken against.

I had but poor help from the old soldier and I had them all to contend with, but when I was like to be run down I bothered them with latitudes and longitudes and the old soldier swore to all I said and we contrived to keep our ground, for we had both been great travellers. When they spoke of heavy taxes I talked of China. When they complained of hard times I told them of West Indian slaves—but neither could make any impression on the other.

When Murray was pressed and I was forced to skulk like a thief, they thought they had a great triumph over me and did not spare their taunts. One would ask what I thought of British freedom; another if I could defend a government which did such things?

I was at no loss for my answer. I told them, 'Necessity had no law.' Could the government make perfect seamen as easily as they could soldiers there would be no such thing as pressing of seamen, and that I was happy to be of more value than them all put together, for they would not impress any of them, they were of so little value compared with me.

When the news of the victory of Trafalgar arrived

I had my triumph over them in return. None but an old tar can feel the joy I felt. I wrought none the next day but walked about enjoying the feeling of triumph. Every now and then I felt the greatest desire to hurra aloud, and many an hurra my heart gave that my mouth uttered not.

For eleven years I lived at Cousland. Year followed year, but still no views of peace. I grew old apace and the work became too heavy for me. I was now fifty-eight years of age, and they would not have taken me had I wished to enter the service. I therefore removed to Edinburgh, and again began to work for myself. My first employers had failed in business long before. The times were completely changed. I could not get constant employment for myself. I therefore wrought for any of the other masters who were throng, but the cooper business is so very poor I have been oftener out of employment than at work. Few of them keep journeymen. They, like myself, do all their work with their own hands.

I never had any children by my cousin during the seventeen years we lived together. Margaret during all that time never gave me a bad word or made any strife by her temper—but all have their faults. I will not complain, but more money going out than I by my industry could bring in has now reduced me to want in my old age.

At her death, which happened four years ago, I was forced to sell all my property except a small room in which I live, and a cellar where I do any little work I

am so fortunate as obtain. This I did to pay the
expenses of her funeral and a number of debts that
had been contracted unknown to me. As my poverty
will not allow me to pay for a seat in a church, I go
in the evenings to the Little Church, but my house is
in the Tolbooth parish.

Doctor Davidson visits me in his ministerial
capacity. These, I may say, are the only glimpses
of sunshine that ever visit my humble dwelling.
Mr Mackenzie, my elder, is very attentive in giving me tickets of admission to the sermons that are
preached in the school house in the Castle Hill.
In one of Doctor Davidson's visits, he made me a
present of a few shillings. It was a great gift from
God. I had not one penny at the time in the house.

In the month of August, last year, a cousin of my
own made me a present of as much money as carried
me to London. I sailed in the *Hawk*, London smack.
I was only a steerage passenger but fared as well as
the cabin passengers. I was held constantly in tow by
the passengers. My spirits were up. I was at sea again.
I had not trode a deck for twenty years before. I had
always a crowd round me listening to my accounts of
the former voyages that I had made. Everyone was
more kind to me than another. I was very happy.

Upon my arrival in London I waited upon my old
captain, Portlock, but fortune was now completely
against me. He had been dead six weeks before my
arrival. I left the house, my spirits sunk with grief for
his death and my own disappointment, as my chief

dependence was upon his aid. I then went to Somerset House for the certificate of my service: seven years in the *Proteus* and *Surprise* in the American War, and seven in the *Edgar*, *Goliah*, *Ramilies* and *Ajax* in the French War.

I was ordered to go to the Admiralty Office first and then come back to Somerset House. When I applied at the Admiralty Office a clerk told me I had been too long of applying. I then went down to the Governor of Greenwich Hospital. I was not acquainted with him, but I knew the Governor of Greenwich would be a distressed seaman's friend. His servant told me he was in Scotland. I then waited upon Captain Gore whose son's life I had saved, but he was not at home. It was of no use to remain in London as my money wore down apace. I took my passage back to Edinburgh in the *Favourite*, London smack, and arrived just four weeks from my first setting out on this voyage of disappointment. What can I do? I must just take what fortune has still in store for me.

At one time, after I came home, I little thought I should ever require to apply for a pension, and therefore made no application until I really stood in need of it.

I eke out my subsistence in the best manner I can. Coffee made from the raspings of bread (which I obtain from the bakers) twice a day is my chief diet. A few potatoes or anything I can obtain with a few pence constitute my dinner. My only luxury is tobacco

which I have used these forty-five years. To beg I never will submit. Could I have obtained a small pension for my past services, I should then have reached my utmost earthly wish and the approach of utter helplessness would not haunt me as it at present does in my solitary home. Should I be forced to sell it, all I would obtain could not keep me and pay for lodgings for one year. Then I must go to the poor's house, which God in his mercy forbid. I can look to my death bed with resignation but to the poor's house I cannot look with composure.

I have been a wanderer and the child of chance all my days, and now only look for the time when I shall enter my last ship, and be anchored with a green turf upon my breast, and I care not how soon the command is given.

SERVICE OF JOHN NICOL

SHIPS' NAMES.	WHERE.	PERIOD.
Proteus and *Surprise*	American War, West Indies	1776–83
Leviathan	Greenland	1784
Cotton Planter	West Indies	1784–85
King George	South Seas and China	1785–88
Lady Juliana	New South Wales and China	1789–91
Amelia	South Sea	1791–92
Nottingham	China	1793–94
Edgar, Goliah, Ramilies and *Ajax*	French War, Egypt, Mediterranean	1794–1801

Index

Collis, Lieutenant 163, 172
Conder (island) 35
Cook, Captain James 12, 80, 83, 99, 116
Cook's River, Alaska 85–6, 97
Corsica 169
Cotton Planter 193
Cousland 185, 186, 189
Currie, Scotland 23

Dalkeith 186, 187
Davidson, Dr (minister) 190
Davis, Ann 116–17
Davis, Deborah 116, 117
Defiance 164
Dick, Sir John, son of 95
Dickson (crewman on *King George*) 12, 83, 96, 98–9
Dickson, Mr (quarryman) 185–6, 187–8
Dixon, Captain 77, 98
Dorset, Sarah 117–18
Duke de Chartres 50, 175
Duncan, Admiral 163
Dundas, Lieutenant Ralph 26
Dutch Folly (fort, Canton, China) 161

Edgar 20, 163–5, 183, 191, 193
Edgar, Lieutenant 116, 123
Edinburgh 2, 4, 10, 15, 17, 19, 175, 183–90, 191–2
Edmonstone 187
Egypt 22, 173, 178–9, 193
England 110, 130, 131–2, 135, 137, 147, 152, 158,
162–3, 180, 183
Equator, crossing the 127–8
Europa 47

Falkland Islands 6, 78–9, 136
Falls of Morant 35
Favourite 191
Ferrel, Elizabeth (Nance) 122, 123–4
Ferrol 178
Firth of Forth 184, 186
Fish, Elizabeth 118
Foley, Captain 172, 173, 174, 175
French Island (Canton, China) 106
French Revolutionary Wars 8, 10, 14–15, 152, 191, 193

Gaspé Bay 35–6
Gibraltar 169, 177, 180
Glasgow and Paisley Packet 24
Goliah 14, 20, 166, 170–1, 172–7, 191, 193
Gore, Captain 191
Gore, Captain (son of) 95, 191
Grant, Gordon 4
Gravesend 152–3
Greenland 60–1, 193
Greenwich, Governor of 191
Grenada 65–74
Guardian 8, 113, 128

Hawaii *see* Owhyee
Hawaiian Islands *see* Sandwich Islands

Montevideo 141
Monts Bay, Cornwall 51
Murray (neighbour at
    Cousland) 186, 188
Musselburgh 186

Nanbaree (Aboriginal) 8, 129
Naples 176
Napoleonic Wars 15–16, 185
Nelson, Admiral 172
New South Wales 113,
    129–30, 135
New York 27–8
Newcastle 55, 57
Newgate Prison 116, 117
Nicol (father) 23–4, 57
Nicol (mother) 23
Nicol, John 1–2, 4–5, 6–15,
    16–18, 19, 22–9, 33–42,
    45–51, 55–62, 65–74,
    77–89, 93–100, 103–10,
    113–32, 135–44, 147–54,
    157–66, 169–80, 183–92,
    193
Nicol, Margaret (wife) 15,
    16, 17, 185, 186, 189–90
Niihau *see* Onehow
Noah, Captain 49–50
Nootka 95, 99
Nootka Sound 13, 22, 96,
    97, 98
Nore 26, 27, 135–6
Norway 163
Nottingham 154, 157–8, 163,
    183, 193

O'Hara, Governor 35–6
Onehow (island) 84–5, 99

Orleans (island) 35
Owhyee (island) 1, 12, 80–3,
    96–7, 98, 99
Owhyee, King of 81

Paita 140–4
Palmer, Henry 120
Parker, George 139
Pitt, William, daughter of
    120–1
Poinoue (son of Abenoue) 99
Port Jackson 1, 8, 9, 116,
    121, 124, 127, 128, 129,
    130, 135, 138, 139
Portlock, Captain 17, 77, 79,
    80, 81, 82, 86, 88, 94–6,
    99, 113, 183, 190
Portsmouth 28, 38
Portuguese vessel 147–50
Powell, Edward 118
Power, William 118
Prince William's Sound
    86–9, 93–5, 97
Proteus 27–8, 29, 37, 38–9,
    45, 171, 191, 193

Quebec 28
Queen Charlotte 77, 80, 98

Ramilies 20, 178, 191, 193
Reeves, Captain 45, 46,
    47–9, 50, 51
Revel, Captain 48, 49
Rhodes 178
Rio de Janeiro 127, 128, 129,
    135, 147, 148
Robinson, Captain 27, 28,
    29, 36

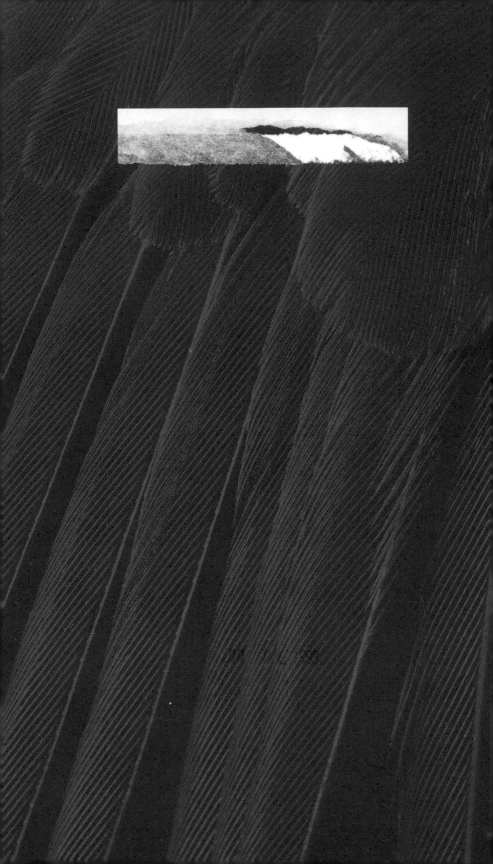